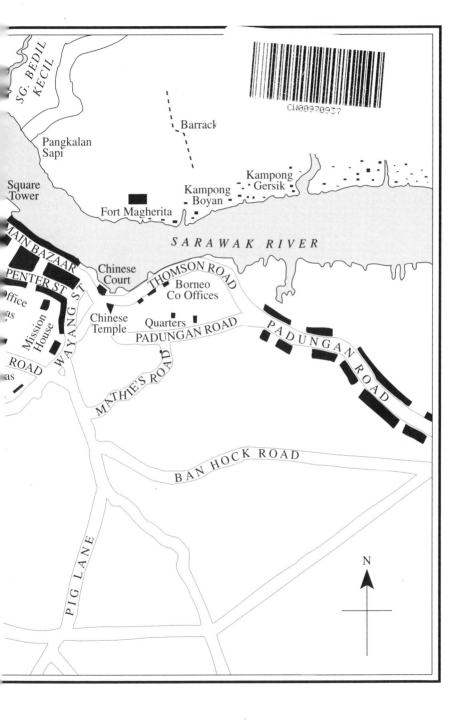

IMAGES OF ASIA

Old Kuching

*Titles in the series*

# Old Kuching

ALICE YEN HO

KUALA LUMPUR
OXFORD UNIVERSITY PRESS
OXFORD SINGAPORE NEW YORK
1998

*Oxford University Press*

*Athens Auckland Bangkok Bogotá Buenos Aires*
*Calcutta Cape Town Chennai Dar es Salaam Delhi*
*Florence Hong Kong Istanbul Karachi*
*Madrid Melbourne Mexico City Mumbai*
*Nairobi Paris São Paulo Shah Alam Singapore*
*Taipei Tokyo Toronto Warsaw*

*and associated companies in*
*Berlin Ibadan*

*Oxford is a trade mark of Oxford University Press*

*Published in the United States*
*by Oxford University Press, New York*

*British Library Cataloguing in Publication Data*
*Data available*

*Library of Congress Cataloging-in-Publication Data*
*Ho, Alice Yen, 1948–*
*Old Kuching/Alice Yen Ho.*
*p. cm.—(Images of Asia)*
*Includes bibliographical references and index.*
*ISBN 983 56 0050 3*
*1. Kuching (Sarawak)—History. I. Title. II. Series.*
*DS597.39.K8H7 1998*
*959.5′4—dc21*
*98-4302*
*CIP*

*Typeset by Indah Photosetting Centre Sdn. Bhd., Malaysia*
*Printed by KHL Printing Co. (S) Pte. Ltd., Singapore*
*Published by Penerbit Fajar Bakti Sdn. Bhd. (008974-T)*
*under licence from Oxford University Press*
*4 Jalan Pemaju U1/15, Seksyen U1, 40150 Shah Alam,*
*Selangor Darul Ehsan, Malaysia*

*To my husband James, for his love and care,*
*and our daughters Tricia and Cynthia, with love*

*... the old times were best. Even I have sailed with Lanun men, and*
*boarded in the night silent ships with white sails. That was before an*
*English Rajah ruled in Kuching.*

Joseph Conrad, *Almayer's Folly* (1895)

# Preface

As the plane approaches Kuching one gets a bird's-eye view of sections of the land from the cabin windows. In the distance the Santubong Mountain and Matang range come into sight, each one a picture on canvas. Below, the rivers are flat ribbons, the colour of milky tea winding leisurely through green surroundings of nipa. Until the early 1960s, the ordinary means of travelling to Kuching had been the steamship services. European travellers, arriving after two days in the vast emptiness of the South China Sea, made much of their first sight of the Borneo coast. They were enchanted by the blue translucence of the mountains—'as if carved from ice'—and the 'green emerald forests' covering the limestone hills. Regular steamers would bypass the westward entrance of the Sarawak River where the Santubong Mountain stands, and choose the wider Muara Tebas on the eastward side to sail into Kuching. Large steamers would wait at this larger river mouth to ride on the swift currents of the swelling tide. Steaming upriver, the captain would find piloting signboards that indicated the deeper water channel to take, the side to keep away from, and the direction to follow to Kuching. Later, they would berth at a wharf called Pending, situated about 1.6 kilometres from the Kuching town centre.

All these seem outdated in this era of airbuses and jumbo jets, but as a child in the 1950s I would arrive in Kuching from Miri in this mode of travel. The name 'Pending' aptly sums up the situation where goods were held at the wharf pending shipment. My earliest recollection of Kuching was a week's stay pending to board another steamer to Singapore, my mother's homeland. We would visit my paternal grandmother who lived in a shophouse (where they said I was born) on Wayang Street just below the St Mary's School ground. For breakfast at my uncle's house where we stayed, there were an assortment of *nonya kuay* (sweet and savoury rice cakes). These were brought to the door by itinerant sellers calling out their wares. Our relatives swore that there were no equals to Kuching's *nonya* food either in Singapore or in Miri.

We were always treated to many tales about the town and its people. Vaguely, it sounded like a Rajah was still living in the Astana when elderly relatives referred to the old Rajah's time, or in jest, talked about getting the Rajah's permission. For inquisitive children like me, a special reason was given for the town's name— that it came from the shape of one of the hills that resembled a cat sitting at rest.

My adult impression of the capital in the 1960s was heightened by the realization that almost everything, even the people's way of life, had seemed to remain as they were 100 years ago: the crooked and uneven five-foot ways of Carpenter and Ewe Hai Streets; the old temples and their *wayang* (opera) stage for holding performances in honour of the deities; boatmen rowing people across the river to get to the kampongs on 'the opposite bank'; and the busy markets where buses, cars, and people mill round each other. I was impressed by the neatness of the town despite its age. I would catch glimpses of the Santubong Mountain or the Matang range in the distance while driving along the undulating ground. Like a scenic backdrop on stage, these hills would dramatically disappear from sight when the rain falls in sheets over Kuching. I planned to live and work in Kuching after my overseas studies. However, my studies and career have taken me to all other destinations except Kuching. Writing *Old Kuching* has given me an insight into the fascinating elements that shaped the capital.

It is impossible to contain every historical detail of Kuching in a single volume. In this book, my main aim is to concentrate on the human element that is so vital in giving this town its distinct character. The book has benefited much from the *Sarawak Gazette* and the *Sarawak Museum Journal*, the numerous Brooke historians, and friends' encouragement.

In acknowledgement, I wish first to thank Noor Azlina Yunus who has been a constant source of my inspiration. Thanks to my longstanding friends, Datuk George Chan Hon Nam, Deputy Chief Minister of Sarawak, and Datin Judith Chan, I was able to start off my ground research in Kuching. My heartfelt thanks for their help, and generous hospitality during my innumerable trips to Kuching. Many thanks to Datuk Lucas Chin, retired curator of the Sarawak Museum, for introducing me to the use of illustrations from the museum's archive. My appreciation to the then acting curator of the Sarawak Museum, Mr Ipoi Datan, for his kind permission to use the photographs, and to Mr Ahmad Junaid Latif and Mr Lim Yu of the photography archive for their assistance. My sincere thanks go to Ms Tan Yong Hiok, assistant curator of the Sarawak Museum, and the librarian Nora Safiee for their friendly assistance and patience. To Julie Yeo at Antiques of the Orient, thanks for kindly providing my illustration needs again. My appreciation goes to Haji Zainuddin bin Sahari at the Miri Public Library for his friendly assistance, and to Mr Lau Yi Bin for lending me Craig Lockard's book, so indispensable to the study of old Kuching. My heartfelt thanks to my relatives and friends in Kuching who have generously given their time, particularly Ho Yam Chin, Tien Chen Yih and Mary Chan Bee. To my husband, my deepest appreciation for sponsoring this project with great patience, and for sharing the love and memories of his old home town. Lastly, I would like to once again thank the Friends of the National Museum of Singapore for sharing the opportunities of learning. *Old Kuching* has had these friends' warm thoughts and good wishes all along.

*Miri*
*March 1998*

ALICE YEN HO

# Contents

# 1

# A Kampong in Borneo

We dropped [anchor] up the river ... to the town of Kuchin (or
Cat Town), the distance is thirty-five miles or thirty-seven miles
(from the river mouth), the water generally deep, but here and
there were awkward rocks.

(James Brooke, Private Letters to John C. Templer, 20 August
1839)

SARAWAK in the early nineteenth century was a south-western
district of the Brunei Sultanate that encompassed the long northern coastal stretch of Borneo. Kuching was one of several Malay
kampongs situated on the Sarawak River inland of this swampy
coastal basin (Plate 1). It began its written history as the capital of
the independent state of Sarawak on 15 August 1839 when James

1. Kuching town in the early 1840s as illustrated by Frank Marryat.
(Sarawak Museum)

Brooke, an English gentleman of some wealth, sailed upriver in his armed schooner, the *Royalist* (Colour Plate 1). In his journal, James Brooke recorded his impression of the kampong that was to become the seat of his government for 100 years. It was 'a little town with brown huts and long-houses made of wood or the hard stems of the nipah palm, sitting in brown squalor on the edge of mudflats' (J. Brooke, 1842).

At the north-west mouth of the Sarawak River, around the foot of the Santubong Mountain, lay the villages of the Malay and Melanau fishermen, and bartering traders. Thirty-two kilometres upriver from Kuching's present site were pockets of settlements occupied by Chinese (Hakka) farmers who had drifted across the Dutch East Indies border (from Sambas). Futher in the interior districts, longhouses built by Land and Sea Dayaks could be found.

A trading settlement of Malay élite, the *datu* and their aristocratic followers, was established at Lidah Tanah (Tongue of Land) 16 kilometres upriver from Kuching. These Malays had found antimony ore here in the early 1820s, and had employed the Land Dayaks and the Chinese to mine for this at Siniawan, 9.5 kilometres from Lidah Tanah. This activity drew the attention of the reigning Brunei Sultan, Omar Ali Saiffudin II, who swiftly sent a *pengiran* (noble) as government representative to Sarawak. In 1826, Pengiran Indera Makhota settled in Santubong, but pirate menace caused him to move to Kuching's present site. His presence, and his action in collecting taxes and stealing from the Dayak inhabitants disrupted the authority of the Malay *datu*, who, as local chiefs, had hitherto been taxing the Dayaks, and trading salt, cloth, and iron with them. In 1836, the Malays, led by Datu Patinggi Ali, allied with the Land Dayaks, and rose against Makhota. They threatened to declare independence and secretly sought help, though unsuccessfully, from the Dutch government in Sambas. The 'rebellion' dragged on for three years, during which the rebels built a wooden stockade, Fort Belidah, across from Siniawan at the foot of the Serambau Mountain. In the same year, the Brunei Sultan sent Rajah Muda Hassim (the heir apparent) to Kuching to resolve the political impasse. Hassim came with his fourteen brothers and their

2

families, and their sizeable entourage of followers and servants, and swelled up the kampong population. Among their spacious houses on the north bank of the Sarawak River was a rambling 'palace' of wood and nipa built for the royal family. In 1839, in the customary open audience hall at the front of the palace facing the river, James Brooke was courteously received by Hassim and his brothers, of whom Badruddin was to become his close friend (Colour Plate 2). In 1841, in the same hall, Hassim proclaimed Brooke the Rajah of Sarawak for rendering him the service of quelling the rebellion.

## Waterways, Pirates, and Inhabitants

Like all the other larger waterways of Borneo, the Sarawak River originates in the interior highlands that form the natural border between Sarawak and the Indonesian part of Borneo. It descends to the hilly rain forests where the migrating Dayaks dwell, and which was known to early Europeans as the Dayak interior. The river reaches the Kuching basin burdened with top soil, logs, jungle debris, and the refuse of the dwellers along its banks. William Hornaday, a British naturalist visiting Kuching in 1878, wrote that the river needed skimming, straining, and filtering. Nevertheless, the transported soil served to 'build up and incessantly enlarge the low land plains', which seem to self reclaim over time as the river enters the sea in a network of deltas and river mouths.

The daily tides of the Sarawak River flow and ebb every six hours with a rise and fall of 4.8 metres along Kuching town's embankments. The Malays living in settlements up to 80 kilometres or more upriver were guided by these tidal rhythms, and by the rainy north-east monsoon from November to March, and the south-west monsoon from May to October. Besides fishing and some rice planting, early Malay peasants also took to collecting, transporting, and bartering the rich mangrove produce from the coasts, and the jungle goods brought out by the Dayaks. The coast-lines of the whole archipelago region are indented with similar sandy river mouths and countless mangrove creeks and bays in their deltaic formations. Until the late nineteenth century, these inlets had provided havens for the formidable pirates that roved the uncharted seas. Notorious for their ferocity and their egregious activities were the Ilanun and Balagnini who hailed from the swampy lagoons of Mindanao and the Sulu islands (Plate 2). They roamed the seas in fleets of *prahu* (long boats) manned by hundreds of fighting men wielding lethal weapons and heavy arms. Boats plying the coast and villagers living in the coastal settlements were victims of their plunders.

2. An Ilanun Pirate. (Frank Marryat, *Borneo and the Indian Archipelago*, 1848)

The Brunei Sultanate was part of the vast Indonesian archipelago that had come under the Indianized empires of the Sri Vijaya and the Majapahit from the seventh to the sixteenth centuries. Archaeological finds from Santubong and its neighbouring areas have proved these early Hindu influences. On the other hand, the Dayak and the coastal Melanau people's hoarding of heirloom ceramic jars have amply documented northern coastal Borneo's claim to strong trade ties with China from the eighth to the fourteenth century. When the Majapahit empire declined in the fifteenth century, the Brunei Sultanate flourished on its own. It was by then a wealthy Muslim state, converted by Arab traders and Indonesian Muslim immigrants. By the early 1800s however, its power had so declined that its Sultan was but a nominal ruler dependent on the Pengirans, the local Malay chiefs, and the Arab Sharifs to collect tributes from the riverine settlements. These 'officers' were empowered to collect an annual 'door' tax of one *pasu* or 22 kilograms of husked rice. Here, a door refers to a family in the Dayak longhouse. Often they would inflate the tax, and reluctantly submit a portion of it to the Sultan, if at all. Indeed, it was known that the farther away the district was situated from the Brunei capital, the more independence it enjoyed. Hence, by the 1830s, the Malays at Lidah Tanah had been more or less masters of their own domain for a few decades. Mukah, Bintulu, and Oya on the north-eastward coast were more heavily taxed, being closer to Brunei; '... the provinces immediately about the capital bear the chief brunt of the Sultan's expenses' (Mundy, 1848).

A large concentration of Malays dwell in the First Division, that is, generally in villages at river mouths, such as at Santubong, and at the point where a tributary meets a main river. The Lidah Tanah was an example of the latter. There the Malay traders controlled the shipping routes from mid-river into the interior, or downriver to the coast. Another heavy concentration of Malays is found in the Limbang and Baram districts that border the present Brunei Sultanate in the north-west. The Bisaya, Kayan, Kenyah, Muruts, Kelabits, and the Penans—collectively designated the Orang Ulu, or people of the upland—dwell in the interior of this northern region. They are dry-padi cultivators, collectors of jungle produce, and hunters, and, excepting the nomadic Penans, live in traditional longhouses. (They originated from central Indonesian Borneo, like the Sea and Land Dayaks.) The Melanaus, or *a Liko*—people of the river—of the Oya and Mukah coastal areas had been established in the sago industry and the fishing occupation from the sixteenth century to the present. The sago paste, scraped from the pith of sago-palm logs and roughly processed, was bartered to the traders, who took them to sago processing factories in Singapore, and later in Kuching. (Refined sago flour was exported to textile and food manufactories in Britain.) Another riverine tribe, the Kedayan, and a majority of the Melanaus are Muslim converts through intermarriages with the Brunei Pengirans, the Arab Sharifs, and the Nakhodas. These latter were popular wealthy traders and boat owners from Sumatra and Malaya who for centuries had frequented the Borneo coasts. A minority of Melanaus are either pagans or Christian converts.

Southwards, along the complex tributaries of the Rejang and Batang Lupar are the Ibans or Sea Dayaks who had migrated from Indonesian Borneo more than 300 years ago. Like the Orang Ulu, these longhouse dwellers and hunters were in constant search of fresh lands to practise their slash–and–burn agriculture. The early Europeans called them 'Sea Dayak' because they were intrepid sailors of *prahu* over rapids and rivers, and were at times seafarers. Among the Ibans were the Saribas and Skrang headhunters who fought the early Brooke government for curtailing their head-taking tradition. The most renowned of these Iban warriors was Rentap ('Earth Tremor'), who fought James Brooke for twenty years. All Dayak groups had the tradition of proving their bravery by taking their enemies' heads at battle times. The urge to accomplish this heroic feat degenerated in the early 1800s (among the more aggressive Ibans) into the indiscriminate 'hunt' for heads. The Iban tradition of *berjalai*—to go away—was once required of every youth entering manhood to sojourn somewhere. On going home, he would prove his worthiness and bravery to the maiden whom he was courting with the acquisition of at least a head 'trophy'. Following this tradition was the Dayak feature of keeping a long lock of hair at the nape to facilitate proper 'handling' if and when his own head was taken (M. Brooke, 1913).

The 'Land Dayaks' were the numerous Dayak groups who perched their villages on almost inaccessible precipices in the in-terior of the First Division. They are now known as the Bidayuh, or people of the interior, and have since lived on lower lands. In the pre-Brooke period, these people had never seen the sea or gone in a *prahu*. After settling into the First Division, they had pur-sued a sedentary agricultural life. By the early 1800s their head-hunting pursuit was limited to battle times with the Iban headhunter enemies. The latter were regularly exploited by the Malay chiefs and Sharifs to raid the Land Dayak longhouses; the headhunters would have the enemies' heads, the chiefs would have the goods, women as captives, and children as slaves. The Land Dayaks, and some gentler Iban tribes settling in the First Division, were to become James Brooke's loyal friends and allies around Kuching. The Skrang and Saribas Ibans were subdued in the 1850s to become his 'army' at large in the Batang Lupar waterways (Plate 3).

The Hakka Chinese had since the early 1700s worked and lived in a semi–autonomous *kongsi* system in various sultanate towns of Dutch Indonesian Borneo. Most of them married the Iban women

3. Skrang Sea Dayaks. (Odoardo Beccari, *Wanderings in the Great Forests of Borneo*, London, Archibald Constable & Co. Ltd., 1904)

as Chinese women were banned from leaving China until the 1890s. The children of these intermarriages were brought up as Chinese, and the Hakka communities maintained their Chinese culture through the regular addition of kin and clan from China. Like all early Chinese immigrants to Nanyang (which translates as the 'Southern Ocean', but designates the coastal region of the archipelago), these goldminers worked with the goal of returning to China to retire in comfort and dignity. In the First Division they settled in the Bau district, 16 kilometres upriver from Lidah Tanah, in a mining and farming community styled after their former Indonesian *kongsi*. Led by a respected elder, they leased settlement rights from the rajahs or chiefs to whom they paid taxes for exporting the minerals, and importing opium. By the 1840s the Bau community had about 2,000 goldminers and families with a leader named Liew Shanbang. They were to come into conflict with James Brooke in 1857 (Chapter 2), when the latter, as the Rajah, fined them for evading taxes, and for hiding a secret society member from Singapore who was then sought after by the Brooke government.

## *James Brooke: The First White Rajah*

James Brooke, born in 1803 in India, was the son of a British civilian in the East India Company (Colour Plate 3). He left school early and joined the company in 1819. In 1825 he was wounded in the Burmese war, and went on a long furlough during which he read avidly about the Far East. After he resigned from the East India Company, he made excursions to Penang, Singapore, Hong Kong, and Canton. In 1835 he inherited his father's wealth, with which he bought the 142-ton burden, the *Royalist*. Although he had read much about Borneo, and yearned to abolish its coastal piracy, it was only when he was in Singapore in 1838 that he determined his course to Sarawak. In Singapore he saw antimony ore being imported from Sarawak by two Armenian merchant firms. The Europeans were paying a high price for antimony, used with lead in manufacturing bullets, in making printing types, and for the new food canning technology. The Brunei aristocrats had used it as a cosmetic, while in Indonesia it was used as a metallic paint on their fabrics. The mineral was known as *serawak* in Malay, and this same name was used on the river that connected to Kuching, and on the district, that is, Sarawak.

Before James Brooke's arrival in Singapore, Hassim in Kuching had ordered the rescue of the crew of a British ship, carrying 2,000 pikuls of antimony ore, that had sunk off the coast. Immensely grateful for this kindness, the European merchants in Singapore persuaded James Brooke to sail to Sarawak and deliver a letter to Hassim. It was an easy persuasion, for James Brooke was curious to see the Malays and Dayaks in rebellion. Having dabbled in trade, he was eager to find the source of the antimony. After visiting Hassim, and meeting and befriending the Dayaks in the interior, James Brooke left Kuching to its curfews, and sailed to the Celebes. He returned in late 1840 to find Hassim pleading for his help to quell the rebellion so he could return to Brunei (where his regency was at stake). He offered to make James Brooke the rajah of Sarawak if he succeeded. With this promise before him, James Brooke led an armed force of 600 Dayaks, Malays, and Chinese to Fort Belidah and ended the protracted warfare. Through James Brooke's diplomacy, the Malay *datu* were forgiven and their lives spared by the Brunei Sultan. In gratitude, the Malay *datu* and the Dayaks wanted to make James Brooke their rajah. However, Hassim hesitated as there was displeasure and opposition from Makhota and the other courtiers. He kept silent about this for months.

In September 1841, James Brooke lost his patience. The *Royalist*, armed with six-pounders and swivel guns, carrying four boats, and flying the white ensign of St George with a red cross, was moored in front of Hassim's palace. With the firearms aimed at his living quarters, Hassim duly signed the transfer of power and proclaimed James Brooke the Rajah of Sarawak. In 1843 Makhota left Kuching in ignominy. Hassim and his clan returned to Brunei in 1845. Thus began the Brooke raj; 'a complex civilization made up of Chinese goldminers, Malay princes and fishermen, Dyak pirates and headhunters had fallen into his hands' (Payne, 1986).

Kuching kampong sprang into a capital town almost instantly on 24 September 1841. James Brooke's jurisdiction, known as Sarawak Proper, only stretched from Cape Datu to the Sadong River, a waterway border with the present Second Division. Frederick Boyle wrote in *Adventures Among the Dayaks of Borneo* (1865) that the town was called by the natives 'Kuching', meaning 'cat', but that 'by Europeans it is frequently called Sarawak'. James Brooke had informally renamed his capital 'Sarawak' in 1842. There was no official acknowledgement on this. The town, country, and river shared the appellation until 1872 when Charles Brooke, his nephew and successor, officially reverted it to 'Kuching' and ended the confusion. 'Kuching' is known to have been derived from Sungei Kuching, a rivulet that flowed past the small Chinese Tua Pek Kong temple at the east end of the town before joining the Sarawak River. The rivulet was named after the *mata kuching*—cat's eye—fruit tree (*Nephelium nalarense*) that flourished on the hill behind the temple, the Bukit Mata Kuching. (The fruit is identical to the *longan* in taste, but is, as its name implies, the size of a cat's eye, and looks like one.) As the First Rajah, James Brooke ruled from 1841 to 1868. He fulfilled his vow to eradicate the coastal piracy; he extirpated headhunting, laid down law and order, and brought peace and trade to Kuching. Warships arriving at Kuching were required to salute the Sarawak flag with twenty-one guns. James Brooke spent his entire fortune and the rest of his life on founding his raj. His repeated offers to Britain to colonize and develop Sarawak were turned down. Under the Second Rajah, Charles Brooke (1829–1917), Sarawak prospered as an independent sovereign state that minted its own coins and postage stamps that bore imprints of the Rajah's face. Charles Brooke, ruling from 1868 to 1917, strengthened his uncle's policies and expanded Sarawak's territories to its present limit at the northern borders with Sabah and Brunei. His son, Vyner Brooke, enjoyed a stable reign from 1917 to 1941. In 1946 Sarawak was ceded to Britain as a crown colony, and Kuching became a colonial capital. In 1963, Sarawak joined the Federation of Malaysia. As the capital of the largest state, Kuching differs in various ways from many other Malaysian towns and cities. Its historical and urban development bears the unique stamp of 'its legacy of a hundred years of rule by the Brooke rajahs' (Lockard, 1987).

# 2
# A Capital Town

*If without mentioning its breadth, I were to state that Kuching extends three-quarters of a mile along either bank of the river, I should give ideas of a magnificence to which the capital, prosperous though it be, has not yet attained.*

(Frederick Boyle, *Adventures Among the Dayaks of Borneo*, 1865)

WHILE the new Rajah was setting up his government, Kuching town began its vigorous growth on both banks of the Sarawak River. In 1843, James Brooke moved from a simple Malay wooden house to Makhota's bungalow on the north bank. It was a 'lofty structure' surrounded by broad verandas, to which he gave the English name, The Grove. He decorated it with native and European weapons of war, and built a library that was worthy of 'a treasure in the jungle'. The Grove sat on a grassy mound, flanked on two sides by the Sungei Bedil Kecil and Sungei Bedil Besar, two streams that would swell into small rivers at high tide. A path led down the rolling ground to a landing place on the main river. On this government residential grounds were coconut and areca palms, fruit trees, and fragrant flowering bushes, including the Rajah's favourite roses. A larger house replaced The Grove on the same site in 1852, and was prosaically named Government House (Colour Plate 4). The Rajah's view of his growing capital across the river took in the small but constantly active Chinese and Indian bazaars, the Malay kampong houses, and the glorious sunset behind the hazy-blue Matang (900 metres) mountain range that lies south-west of the town.

## The Old Town Core

The town would awake every morning to the hustle and bustle of two markets on the bank opposite the Rajah's residence. These were atap-roofed sheds where the population made their daily purchases of meat, fruits, and vegetables. Further left from the markets, a rivulet called Sungei Gartak marked the town's west end. A community of Boyanese, brought in from Bawean Island off Java by Hassim, settled in Kampong Jawa between the rivulet and the markets. The Malay *datu* and their noble followers from Lidah Tanah settled south-west of this area, which became the Datu's Kampong. This was the nucleus of a sophisticated class of urban Kuching Malays, the *Perabangan*, or ruler class, from which was culled the *datu* and the main corps of the Brooke government's native officers. A steady immigration of coastal Malay villagers from around Santubong, Samarahan, and Sadong, and Malay Muslims and traders from Sumatra, Java, and Celebes, had begun to stream into Kuching. They formed clusters of self-contained kampongs on the north bank, up and downriver from the government residential grounds. The kampongs were named after their places of origins, or their leaders, like Kampong Surabaya, Kampong Boyan, and Kampong Gersik (of the Minangkabau). A wooden mosque, structured like a Malay dwelling house, sat on a foothill at a bend of the Sarawak River. This served the early Muslims as a place to worship until 1852, when a bigger mosque, the Masjid Besar, was built on the knoll behind to contain a larger and more settled Muslim population.

A small community of Indian Moplah merchants settled south of the markets. They had originated from the Malabar Coast of India, but had probably moved from the large Indian communities of the Straits Settlements. A dirt road, known as Kling Street, ran in front of their wooden shops dealing in Indian textiles, brassware, spices, and market goods. This early 'Little India' community professed the Shiite faith, and worshipped in a wooden prayer hut behind the shops. Hugh Low in *Sarawak: Its Inhabitants and Productions* (1848) observed that although the local Malays were of orthodox Sunni faith, the two sects in Kuching dwelled peacefully in proximity, but that the Malays had never worshipped in the Indian mosque. Kling Street was structurally improved over the decades, and was renamed India Street in 1928 at the request of the larger Indian community (Colour Plate 5).

A wide dirt road running east along the river bank served as a street for a row of rickety, wooden Chinese shophouses. The Main Bazaar, presently Kuching city's oldest thoroughfare, began its existence inadvertently as a wide embankment where traders conveniently loaded and unloaded their goods (Plate 4). It was a track of mud and slush especially when the tides or the monsoon rain flooded the river. At low tide, it was strewn with debris washed up by the tide and sun-rotted fish. At the eastern end of this early Main Bazaar, an atap-roofed fish market stood by Sungei Kuching, and opposite the Tua Pek Kong Temple. In 1928 the rivulet was filled up to yield roads that ran to the rural Padungan district. In 1856, the Borneo Company had planted its warehouses on the

4. Kuching waterfront in 1864 with the shops on Main Bazaar, presently the oldest thoroughfare. (Sarawak Museum)

bank east of the temple, at the foot of the Bukit Mata Kuching. It was the only European commercial enterprise that James Brooke had permitted to operate in the country. Ships steaming upriver towards Kuching town would, after a panorama of miles of nipa palms, pass with relief and delight the lively Malay kampongs on the river banks. The whitewashed Borneo Company warehouses, with a landing for washing and loading antimony ore, would be their first landmark of some 'civilization' ahead.

Shortly south of the Chinese shops, the ground appeared elevated with a seemingly impenetrable jungle. In 1848, the Reverend Francis McDougall (who became Bishop of Sarawak and Labuan in 1855), and his wife Harriette arrived in Kuching (Plate 5). They headed the Borneo Mission (1848–68), a private missionary group later supported by the Society for the Propagation of the Gospel. The Rajah donated 16 hectares of the land to the Mission on which Mission House was built in 1849. The Malay workmen cleared the jungle, flattened the hilltop, and dug the foundation. The St Thomas Cathedral and its small cemetery stood a little down the slope (Colour Plate 6). In the Mission House (now Bishop's House) the McDougalls ran a little day school, which was historically Kuching's first St Thomas and St Mary. Its orphanage began with four 'half caste' children whom the Rajah found 'running about in the bazaar', and ten Chinese Hakka children from a refugee influx in 1850. The Rajah often found it necessary to turn in Dayak and Malay children sent to him as slaves. (Slavery was abolished by Charles Brooke in 1886). The Mission dressed them with clothes made by Chinese tailors in town, fed, and educated them (Plate 6). The Mission House was also a dispensary and hospital where Bishop McDougall, a highly qualified surgeon, tended to the Malays, Dayaks, and a handful of Europeans. The early Chinese made occasional use of the clinic, but they would often have a Chinese physician among themselves, as Harriette McDougall noted.

The early small Chinese population were predominantly from Singapore's major Hokkien and Teochew dialect groups. The prevailing presence of the Hokkiens in town, and their powerful commercial base largely account for the Hokkien dialect being the

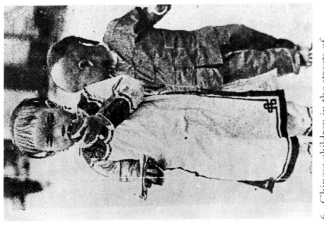

6. Chinese children in the streets of Kuching were clothed and fed by the McDougalls. (Sarawak Museum)

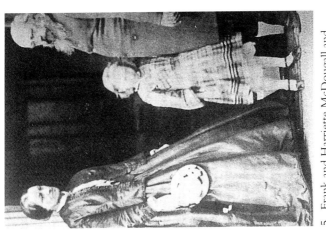

5. Frank and Harriette McDougall and their youngest daughter, Mildred. (Harriette McDougall, *Sketches of Our Life at Sarawak*, Society for Promoting Christian Knowledge, 1882)

patois of Kuching's Chinese inhabitants regardless of their own speech groups. One would also notice that most Indian merchants in Kuching speak Hokkien fluently. The most notable Hokkien trader to come from Singapore in 1846, after Kuching had achieved some peace and stability, was Ong Ewe Hai, who became the first Chinese Kapitan (from the Portuguese 'Capitan' for 'leader'). He started a humble bartering business with the Malays and Dayaks, and this later grew and became the prominent Ong Ewe Hai and Company. Another trader, Lau Kian Huat, was a Teochew who came in 1852 and established Ghee Soon Company. Teochew-speaking traders persistently rivalled the Hokkiens in their similar lucrative trades wherever they settled, although the former's trades were more agriculturally based. In Kuching, both groups dealt in the importation of major grocery goods, and the exportation of sago, gambier (*Unicara gambir*), and pepper, and later, rubber. The robust pepper and gambier trades (of the Teochews) were later concentrated at Kampong Jawa, which developed into Gambier Road and Market Street in the 1880s. (Gambier leaves yield a dye for batik, sail canvas, and for tanning leather; it is also an optional ingredient in the betel chew or *sirih-makan*. Gambier dregs made excellent fertilizer for pepper vines, hence they were twin crops.) A small number of Cantonese artisans and market gardeners lived in Kuching's vicinity in the 1830s. The Rajah's first steward was a Cantonese named Lau Chek who came from Satok (west of Kuching). He is said to have helped the First Rajah hoist St George over Kuching, and fought with him against the Bau goldminers in 1857.

In 1850, about three to four thousand Hakka Chinese, while escaping *kongsi* rival warfare in Sambas, swarmed into Kuching. The refugees camped almost everywhere with their mats and belongings, much to the dismay of the European officers. On one incident, Bishop McDougall came upon a large group sleeping inside their mosquito nettings in the partially completed church building, their tobacco 'perfuming the place' and there were 'nails knocked into the walls to tie up the curtains' (McDougall, 1882). The Rajah, desirous of the economic prospect of their settlement, donated rice and tools so that these refugees could open up the jungles. A large majority joined the Bau goldmining community, or dispersed as rural market gardeners. In Kuching, behind Main Bazaar, a small number of these Hakkas (following the Cantonese artisans) went into carpentry, tin smithery, and tailoring. These activities (including coffin-making) gave Carpenter Street its name.

A road of about 3.2 kilometres led to the immediate Dayak interior. This was known as Rock Road (now Jalan Tun Haji Openg), and 'it was all Kuching then boasted', a highway on which James Brooke used to walk his 'old Arab' in the 1850s (Helms, 1882). Frederick Boyle wrote that an 'enormous wild boar' haunted Rock Road every night, and crossed the Bishop's path on his constitutional ride. From Harriette McDougall's vivid description, one could visualize the Bishop (with his Armenian ancestry) cutting a robust and hilarious figure in town with his flaring beard and priestly robe, and riding a pony named Don. Rajah Charles Brooke and the Ranee used to 'pound' on this road in their horse-riding exercise at six every morning.

Until the 1920s, the Rajah's stables, 'complete with coach-house, harness room and hay-loft', stood at the junction of Rock Road and Carpenter Street (at the present General Post Office site). These were maintained by the renowned Boyanese grooms. Horses, pony carts, and carriages were Kuching's earliest modes of transport for the Rajah, his higher European officers and visitors, the Borneo Company managers, and the *datu*. The population and lower European officers travelled around town on foot, and by sampans, *tambang* (covered boats), and *prahu* on the network of innumerable rivers and creeks. Bullock carts for passengers and for bulky goods were not used until after 1870 when the roads were vastly improved, and bullocks were imported from India. The Dayaks would walk into town with everything in their 'backpack', a long rattan basket. In the bazaars, the Chinese labourers skilfully heaved gunny-sack loads onto their shoulders. Until the 1950s, the Chinese and Malay itinerant food sellers hawked their wares in two bamboo baskets or containers slung in ropes from a wooden pole which they balanced on the shoulders (Plate 7).

In *Ten Years in Sarawak* (1866), Charles Brooke wrote: 'this was all [that Kuching had in 1852], except a stockaded place called a

7. A Chinese hawker with his wares in the baskets slung in ropes from a wooden pole which he balanced on his shoulders. (Sarawak Museum)

fort ... and a court-house on the upper side of the bazaar'. The wooden fort was a six-gun battery surrounded by a moat at a landing place called Pangkalan Batu located directly opposite Government House. A garrison of twenty-five Malays under a native commandant kept a 24-hour surveillance on the river's activities. On ceremonial occasions, and in honour of visiting naval vessels, it would boom forth in gun salutations. The echoes served to inform the nearby Dayaks of the Rajah's movements, whence the news would travel to the interior longhouses. The Dayaks would decide to go to Kuching, to bring their respects or their grievances to their Rajah. An early Iban community in Kuching dwelt in a longhouse in Padungan until 1856 when Ghee Soon Company built the first sago flour processing factory in the area (Colour Plate 7). In 1858, at James Brooke's request, a small community of Balau Ibans from Batang Lupar, settled in a longhouse behind the Chinese area. Their presence was an intimation of the Rajah's fearsome supporters after the 1857 conflict with the goldminers. They were resettled in a larger suburban area 6.4 kilometres south, that subsequently became Kampong Tabuan, a pioneer community of Kuching's urban Iban society. Prominent

18

Ibans of Kuching today trace their roots back to Jangun, the Balau leader who delivered the Rajah's message of Kuching's predicament to Charles Brooke in the Second Division.

James Brooke had administered his early government in the large audience and dining hall of The Grove. In 1848, after he was knighted, he moved his informal court to the ground floor of an abandoned two-storey wooden school building behind the Pangkalan Batu fort. In this first 'Court House', he officially presided over all hearings and litigation with his two European assistants and three Malay *datu* in attendance. Thus, the tradition began for the Rajah to cross the river to get to his office on the south bank. At each embarkation and disembarkation, a Royal Umbrella Bearer would hold a large yellow satin umbrella over the Rajah's head (Plate 8). This stately umbrella was a symbol of Malay aristocracy that was adopted for use at all official functions and ceremonies throughout the three Rajahs' reigns.

## *The River: Highway and Thoroughfare*

Unassumingly, the Sarawak River, cutting through the centre of the roadless township, assumed the role of the main thoroughfare. Malay and Dayak *prahu* came in with rattan, salted fish, beeswax, sago paste, sharkfins, birds' nests, and sundry jungle and mangrove produce to barter with the Chinese shopkeepers. Chinese trade junks berthed on the river, unloading several Chinese immigrants from Singapore or China. Monthly schooners from Singapore tooted signals of mail from England; boats and frigates unloaded goods and loaded the antimony ore, and the jungle produce. Hugh Low noted that Kuching imported 'salt, opium (consumed by the Chinese), silks, cocoa-nut oil, brass wire, and brass cooking pots ... Javanese handkerchiefs, and European cloths and earthenware, and also much of the coarser earthen manufacture of China'.

Kuching's political atmosphere before 1846, and the Rajah's policy of keeping at bay large manufacturing enterprises that would exploit the natives and the Chinese for labour, were not conducive to attracting a large population settlement or a brisk trade. The Ilanun and Balagnini pirates continued their coastal

8. A Sarawak Ranger officer holding a large yellow satin umbrella over the Rajah's head. (Sarawak Museum)

menace, at times pulling into Kuching to scout the place. At other times, sleek *prahu* of the Skrang and Saribas headhunters would skim silently into town. Hoping that the White Rajah would relent, they would seek 'licence' to raid the Dayak villages, like in the old days. Two chiefs named Matahari, 'the Sun', and Bulan, 'the Moon', begged James Brooke for permission to 'steal just a head or two ... or maybe three ...'. The astounded Rajah likened it to how 'a school boy would ask for apples' (J. Brooke, 1842). The river of trade would turn into a rallying ground of hundreds of native war *prahu* whenever the First or Second Rajah (until the 1880s) was fitting out punitive expeditions on the pirates and headhunters (Colour Plate 8). The muddy water of the Sarawak River, filled with colourful war vessels bearing fear-inspiring names, would resound with gunfire. The eerie Dayak war 'yell' that filled the air was described by Charles Brooke as a terrifying experience that 'froze the blood in one's veins'.

Between 1843 and 1850, a concourse or a relay of visiting British men-of-war would elbow for space with the regular trade frigates, junks, sailboats, and schooners. In the centre of this remote kampong town surrounded by thick jungles, the first British gunboat to visit Kuching, the HMS *Dido*, anchored in early 1843. This 18-gun corvette made an awesome picture on the river, with its towering mastheads, and 250 white-uniformed sailors furling sails to music played by a live band. Captain Sir Henry Keppel (1808–1903) proudly witnessed the tumultuous welcome accorded the Rajah by all his subjects on his return from a holiday in Penang. The river was 'covered with canoes and boats dressed out in their various coloured silken flags, filled with natives beating their tom-toms' (Keppel, 1846). In the same year, the HMS *Samarang*, on leaving town after a call, hit a rock in mid-river and ran aground for eleven days (Colour Plate 9). The crew roamed the bazaars and the Rajah's gold and antimony mining districts. They bathed in the streams, which one of the midshipmen, Frank Marryat, found to be infested with 'mischievous' alligators. At night wild hogs, porcupines, wild cats, and other animals visited their lodgings on the north bank.

Marryat sketched some of the finest portraits of Kuching in its 'infancy'. He wrote that there were 'about 800 houses, built on piles into the ground, the sides and roofs being enclosed with dried palm leaves' (Marryat, 1848).

Another striking scene on the river was the town's Royal Proclaimer making his round of duty. Subu was a Malay seaman from the *Royalist*. He was made the first State Executioner for his outstanding physical build and strength, his great composure, and his unmatched skill at using the *keris*. Subu put condemned criminals to their instant end by thrusting the *keris* into the right collar bone, and diagonally through the heart. As the Royal Proclaimer, he would don a blue gold-embroidered jacket with a gold waist band, and a pair of black trousers. A coloured handkerchief on his head was tied 'in a jaunty fashion, with two ends standing up over his left ear'. No less solemnly, he would embark on a long boat that had the Rajah's flag and that was paddled by twenty men. At each jetty he would stop to read the Proclamations (in Malay) to the illiterate population. Like all Brooke officers with their 'poly-responsibilities', Subu was also the Royal Umbrella Bearer until his demise in 1873. The job probably required his stature and stoutness, for Captain Keppel had described the umbrella as a 'huge yellow canopy'.

The same sea water-inundated river that carried jungle debris, trade and war, and the town's sewage was also a source of early Kuching's water supply (from Sungei Gartak). Outbreaks of cholera or dysentery were frequent. An epidemic in 1858 took a few hundred Malay lives, while that of 1888 killed a thousand people in its wake. Charles Brooke noticed that the bazaar Chinese were much less afflicted than the natives. This acute observation might have expedited his government scheme for a town reservoir to store water from the Matang mountains to be piped into the houses. It was likely that he would have read from the late Sir Stamford Raffles' history of eighteenth-century Java that the Chinese there were careful over drinking only boiled water, a process that killed the 'little invisible creatures'. For making tea, or manufacturing tofu and beansprouts, the Kuching Chinese would have used well water and collected rain water. The water supplied to the more affordable households by the Chinese *tukang air*—

water carrier—might have come from a large well in Upper China Street (sealed up in the 1880s), as well as from the Sungei Gartak. Water was transported in two kerosene tins slung from a pole that were balanced over the untiring Chinese shoulders. The river water would be allowed to sit and clarify, and treated before use. The Chinese have always refrained from the native indulgence in raw meat and vegetables. Natives long influenced by the Chinese in older South-East Asian cities eventually acquired the habit of drinking warm boiled water or hot tea, though not the habit of cooking everything. It 'seems likely that Europeans first learned its [boiled water's] advantages ... probably by following the local or Chinese example' (Reid, 1988).

## Security Forces and Devastation

By the mid-1850s, the Batang Lupar's Iban headhunters had become the government's unpaid and irregular army. They responded swiftly to the summons of Charles Brooke, the Tuan Muda (Young Lord), when they received the official dispatch of a spear to them. Kuching's first armed service, the Fortmen, formed in 1846, was a recruit of thirty Dayak and Malay youths from élite families commissioned to guard the forts and the Rajah's residence. The Fortmen were later increased to a hundred and twenty soldiers commanded by Major Rodway, an ex-British army officer. In their white uniforms with black braid trimmings (devised by Charles Brooke), and arms, these soldiers were also barefooted (at least until the 1890s). In 1866, sixty convicted Sepoys from the Indian Mutiny of 1857 arrived from India. They joined the Fortmen to form the Sarawak Rangers in 1872, the first military in Kuching (Plate 9).

However, before the security forces were firmly established, Kuching was devastated by what Brooke historians have called the Chinese Rebellion of 1857. In the early hours of 19 February, about 600 Bau goldminers led by Liew Shanbang took Kuching town by surprise (Plate 10). They overpowered the Fortmen at the Pangkalan Batu fort, killed four Europeans (including beheading and throwing two children into the flames), and burned down two

9. The Sarawak Rangers on parade. (Sarawak Museum)
10. Chinese goldminers from Bau, 32 kilometres upriver from Kuching town. (Sarawak Museum)

of their houses. In the dark, James Brooke swam across the tide-swollen Sungei Bedil Besar and sought refuge in a Malay kampong. The goldminers, mistaking a young Englishman for the Rajah, took his head and paraded it on a pike in town. The Government House was torched, and the Rajah's library burned for two days, 'glowing dull red like a furnace' as the McDougalls watched from the Mission House. At daybreak, Liew Shanbang sat in the Rajah's Court House and summoned the Datu Bandar, Bishop McDougall, a Mr Ruppell, and Mr Ludvig Helms, the Borneo Company manager. He suggested that the Datu rule over the Malays, the Bishop be the Rajah of the Europeans, and his Bau autonomy to oversee Kuching. At the inconclusive meeting, the Bishop reminded the goldminers that the Tuan Muda was 'the Governor of the Sea Dayaks, and could let loose at least 10,000 wild warriors upon them' (St John, 1886). After a cockerel-blood sprinkling oath and tea ceremony, and after looting and threatening the Chinese bazaar, the goldminers left reluctantly on the third day. When some Malays continued to pursue them, the antagonized goldminers returned to destroy the Datu's Kampong and ransack the Mission House. On the fifth day, the Borneo Company's *Sir James Brooke* returned from Singapore, picked up the Rajah from downriver, and stormed into Kuching. The goldminers beat a doomed retreat into Siniawan and Bau, with the Iban army at their heels. Liew Shanbang was killed at a place called Jugan Siniawan on 24 February. Almost none of his two thousand or more goldminers and their families were spared in the pogrom, and those who crossed the border were hounded by the Dutch authorities.

Kuching's Chinese traders, though supportive of the government, nevertheless suffered the immediate aftermath of the catastrophe. The angered Malays found much fault with them. The Dayaks on the other hand, gleefully 'cooked'—smoke-treated—the goldminers' heads in the streets. Many Chinese left the town with all their belongings, in schooners. Charles Brooke wrote that for many years after the incident, 'the population were so nervous that the most frivolous accident occasioned a panic'.

Kuching was left more perturbed than before when an intrigue harboured by Datu Haji Gapur (Datu Patinggi Ali's successor from

25

11. Kuching in the 1860s, on its way to recovery from poverty and catastrophes. (Sarawak Museum)

1844) to overthrow the Brooke government was quickly quelled in 1859. The early 1860s saw a shabby, traumatized Kuching town slowly recovering from the iniquities of war, unrest, and an unstable economy (Plate 11). The Chinese had returned in drifts and were filled with uncertainty about their future. More *kajang* or palm leaf walls, wood, and atap roofs replaced many of the shophouses, earning Carpenter Street its nickname, Atap Street. The few roads remained as beaten tracks and muddy paths. During high tide, the embankments brimmed with all sorts of trading boats and junks. The reflux exposed the stilts of the water-kampong houses, the mangrove roots, and the slippery banks of the markets and trading areas.

In 1868, Kuching mourned the death of their First Rajah who died in England. For a week, the Sarawak flag flew at half mast over the capital. By 1861 Sarawak had encompassed the Mukah and Oya districts.

# 3
## Austerity and Prosperity

Kuching is reclaimed jungle—but thirty years has given it a European look. The streets are clean and wide.

(James Austin Wilder, *Visit to Sarawak*, 1896)

THE 1870s marked a new era for Kuching. The arrival of steam-driven vessels in the Borneo waters brought the coastal piracy under control. The opening of the Suez Canal shortened the trade routes to and from Europe. Mails from Singapore to Kuching now took a mere ten days. Rajah Charles Brooke made the capital changes and improvement that Kuching needed most—its bureau-cratic administration and infrastructure. Under his directives, Kuching became a clean, beautiful town on which visitors bestowed much praise as they expressed awe at its head of state: 'The Rajah is absolute' (Wilder, 1896). He was determined to make his capital a modern town (Colour Plate 10). 'Endlessly puffing at his Manila cheroots, he would order a road built here, a bridge built there, or a new factory for processing oil from areca nuts over there' (Payne, 1966). Charles Brooke had lived and worked in Sarawak since 1852 (Colour Plate 11). He had been but Tuan Muda in name and Rajah in authority since 1863. The ailing Sir James Brooke had retired in England after disinheriting Charles's brother, the Rajah Muda, Johnson Brooke, over the accession dispute. Charles Brooke knew the Kuching bureaucracy in detail, and his familiarity with every civil servant's character and lifestyle was uncanny. His European staff had been described as an *esprit de corps*: they had no family life, and no furlough for the first ten years of their service. He had observed their inclination towards the 'ruler class' when the First Rajah's younger officers (including Johnson Brooke) brought their wives from England. He also noticed how 'withdrawn' the Kuching people were (during their informal calls on the Rajah) when the officers and their female companions retreated to the 'drawing room' for a cup of tea after dinner.

The Second Rajah's personal regimen was no less strict. In *My Life in Sarawak* (1913), the Ranee Margaret Brooke described her husband as the 'most punctual man alive'. His clockwork of a routine was supposedly emulated by all: 'At five o'clock in the morning, just before daybreak ... a gun was fired from the Fort, at which signal the Rajah jumped out of bed. Wishing to do the same as the Rajah, the Europeans, Malays, Dayaks, and Chinese jumped out of bed too.' Another gun fired at eight in the evening served as the Rajah's 'dinner gong'. Known to the Kuching people as the 'eight-o'clock gun' in Hokkien, it continued to boom away each evening until the late 1960s, serving no grander purpose than echoing a charming bygone era.

Commanding neither great stature nor possessing any social grace, Charles Brooke drove both fear and respect into all who knew him; his orders were command, and 'his wishes were laws'. In the sixty-five years of his life in Sarawak, he was loved, revered, and befriended by all. Colonial officers, gauging the people's consent to cede Sarawak to Britain in 1946, found that the elderly Dayaks of the interior would talk about their beloved Second Rajah, whom, they thought, was still residing in Kuching.

## A New Capital

In 1869, the wooden Government House was demolished to give way to the Second Rajah's white fortress-like edifice, the Astana (Colour Plate 12) (see Chapter 6). It was the first brick building in Kuching, and was completed in 1870 to be ready for the arrival of the Ranee Margaret. During his early tenure, Charles Brooke had begun devising various schemes and projects to liven the economy. The Matang estates, modelled on Ceylon's tea estates, set up in 1867, were an experiment in planting tobacco, coffee, and tea for export. The Rajah then began a private dairy business called the Astana Farm on the Astana grounds (Plate 12). It supplied the 'European Officers and civilians ... with pure fresh milk', and provided the town with bullocks for transportation, and the Muslims

**Notice.**

———◆———

**Astana Farm Produce.**
Terms Monthly.

WILL be supplied to customers at the following rates :—

| | | |
|---|---|---|
| Milk—per quart bottle | ... ... | ... 10 cents |
| Butter—per lb ... | ... | ... 80 „ |
| Eggs—each ... | ... | ... 1½ „ |

Orders, which should be addressed to the undersigned, attended to without delay.

J. STAPLES,

12. An advertisement for Astana Farm produce in the *Sarawak Gazette* in 1906. (Sarawak Museum)

and Europeans with the occasional beef from old or indisposed cattle. A present-day reminder of this farm contingency is the cattle's watering spot, known as the Pangkalan Sapi, a jetty where colourful *tambang* load or unload their fares at the Astana ground. The farm closed in 1925 without any impressive economic record, while another enterprise began with a modern dairy production machinery in Padungan. This was closed in 1948.

In 1874, a sprawling complex of one-storey brick buildings replaced the wooden Court House behind Pangkalan Batu. Situated opposite the Astana, the white colonnaded buildings with roofs of belian (ironwood) slates housed an administrative body comprising the court room, the resident's office, treasury, post office, shipping office, audit office, and the government's printing press. Its inauguration ceremony began with endless gun salutes from the fort and the trading boats in the river, and fire crackers in the Chinese bazaar. It ended with the tune of the Sarawak National Anthem (composed by Ranee Margaret in 1872) and more celebratory din from English guns and Chinese fireworks. The crowd that gathered

included 'turbaned Hajis dressed in long gowns of gaudy colors ...
Sepoys and Kling in flowing white garments, the well dressed
pig-tailed celestial, and the unsophisticated Dyak (innocent of dress
bar a waist cloth) ... the whole forming a most interesting assem-
blage' (*Sarawak Gazette*, July 1874).

On weekdays, a daily ritual was held to begin the government
officers' day. The Rajah would arrive in his usual blue serge coat
and white trousers, with a buttonhole of honey suckle and a white
helmet, and armed with his long silver-mounted staff. Arthur Ward
wrote in *Rajah's Servant* (1966):

Behind him a Sergeant of the Sarawak Rangers held aloft a considerably
dilapidated yellow umbrella, while a Malay retainer, carrying books and a
paper umbrella in case of rain, brought up the rear. As the little procession
advanced, guards turned out and presented arms; the Resident ... made a
bolt from his room to greet the Rajah at the portico ...; and the Head
Native Officers, the four Datus, drew up in line to have their hands
shaken. The Rajah then passed on to his office, where he was accessible to
any person, native or European, who wished to see him.

In concurrence with the modernization of the town, the wealth-
ier Hokkien and Teochew *towkay* (merchants) were prompted
to renovate their shabby wooden shophouses on Main Bazaar
(Plate 13). Brick shophouses with roofs of belian shingles began to
appear, giving the Chinese township a scenic look, especially when
viewed from the distance of the boats, and the Astana.

## The Order of the Day

The development of Sarawak, and the current events of Kuching
from 1870 onwards, were recorded in no sparing detail in a monthly
government publication called the *Sarawak Gazette* (Plate 14). Its
first issue in August 1870 announced that it was published 'with a
hope that it may both supply a want in the country, and be of service to those in other places who are interested in the prosperity of
Sarawak and its dependencies'. It endeavoured to publish news of
Europe gleaned from papers received from the steamer mail.
European officers, yearning for news from their homeland soon

13. The Main Bazaar after the renovation of the 1870s.

14. The first issue of the *Sarawak Gazette*, August 1870.
    (Sarawak Museum)

found it bearing reports of Kuching and its districts ('Another alligator caught by Malays above Sarawak [River]'). It carried shipping notices, Supreme Council proceedings, court cases, birth and death announcements, and essays on a wide number of subjects. Until another official government gazette appeared in 1904, the *Gazette* carried the administrative reports of officers working out of the town, solemnly prefaced with 'Rajah, I have the honour to inform Your Highness', and closing with 'Sir, I have the honour to be your obedient servant'. None the less, Vyner Brooke, on the *Gazette's* 1,000th run in 1937, remarked that it '... will be the most accurate and interesting record of Sarawak history as time marches on'.

In a modernizing town, old Subu's royal proclamation at the jetties would have appeared archaic. One of the *Gazette's* expediencies was to carry the Rajah's stipulations and edicts on renovating the town. Sheds or houses of *kajang* walls were ordered to be torn down, and haphazard structures dismantled. In 1871 Atap Street was transformed into a street with 'neat plank houses, roofed with belian, and built with some approach to regularity' (*Sarawak Gazette*, 1871). Large new markets with concrete counters replaced the atap sheds. The Borneo Company's white-washed warehouses were hailed as an example of neatness that gave a first bright impression of the capital's well-being. In its November 1884 issue, the *Gazette* commented on the ungainly contrast of the dingy and mouldy old shops with the newly built. A hint was noted: 'The adoption of the Dutch and we believe, the Spanish plan of compulsory whitewashing once a year would not in any way be a hardship on the people.'

The Main Bazaar's shophouses were constructed with the aim of utilizing its limited lots to yield the maximum number of similar premises. The two-storey shophouses were slim in width, but in length they were about 30.5 metres deep extending right into the back lane (providing ample storage for gunny sacks of grocery goods). They ended with a courtyard that was lit by skylights and fenced in by a high wall. The more affluent shopkeepers would add another floor in later years, and decorate the frontal roofs and walls with Chinese and Malay ornamentation and frescoes. The five-foot ways—*kaki lima*—that sheltered goods and people from the harsh elements of nature were mandatory features that seemed to be an emulation of the colonial shophouses in Singapore and Malaya. Visitors, hoping to catch a glimpse of some Dayaks in full regalia, would instead find themselves winding through the clutter of imported merchandise along these corridors, where sun-shading draperies were 'hung from pillar to pillar'. Imperious orders to unclog the pavements, and remove the stray dogs were issued. Besides, the shopkeepers had further clogged the pavements by stacking firewoods that were used for cooking. These posed as handy lethal weapons when the Teochew and Hokkien trade rivals, sometimes joined by the Henghua fishermen group (see Chapter 5) brawled through the night streets. These clan battles were reined in by the Rajah's order to arrest and flog all parties. (In Kuching, as in Singapore, early Chinese immigrants held governing authorities with contempt, and nicknamed the police constables 'Tua Kow' in Hokkien and Teochew, or 'Anchin Besar' in Malay, meaning 'Big Dog'.)

Shops in side-lanes like China Street and Upper China Street (ending close to the missionary ground and its cemetery) were mainly licensed gambling and opium dens, and arrack shops, three of the biggest sources of revenue for the Brooke government. Like a prophet of doom, the Rajah had expressed grave concern for the poorer sector that was found behind Main Bazaar. The sector was crammed with an assortment of businesses and families. The Rajah's fears were realized when a fire broke out on Carpenter Street one early Sunday morning in January 1884. The flame lapped up more than 130 shophouses, and threatened to burn down the newer Main Bazaar shops, the Rajah's stables, and the Court House. Kuching's Great Fire, as it was called, was finally put out as much by a timely downpour at dawn as by the rather chaotic effort of the Malays, Europeans, and Chinese setting in motion all the fire engines and water buckets in town. The conflagration quickened the town's sprucing up activities. In less than two years, it became mandatory for shophouses to use bricks as building materials. The entrepreneurial Ong Ewe Hai built forty shop lots on a new street named after himself. Ewe Hai Street joins Carpenter Street at Bishopsgate, a side lane with a wooden gate through which the missionaries, and later, boarders from St Mary's School, used in their trips to the town and river.

Towards the early 1900s, Kuching's population grew to 20,000. A varied style of architecture graced the town core. There was the formidable, well-armed Fort Margherita, named after the Ranee, built in 1879 on a strategic knoll of land on the north bank. The potentate of a Court House sat amongst the bazaars. The Square Tower housing a prison replaced the Pangkalan Batu fort. A turret-like building—Round Tower—behind the Court House was built as a dispensary. Beside it was a three-storey building called the Pavilion that served as the medical headquarters (Plate 15). The style of the Pavilion was similar to some of the buildings found in the southern states in America. An impressive Sarawak Museum was built a short distance south of the town centre (see Chapter 6).

15. The Pavilion was built to house the medical headquarters. (Darrell Tsen)

One could also find a golf course, several social clubs, a race course at Padungan, and four schools belonging to the Anglican and Roman Catholic missionaries. Three Chinese temples, a Sikh temple, two mosques, and two cathedrals reflected the multiple faiths of the neat township.

In 1881 the Reverend Father Aloysius Gossens and two other priests came to Kuching to set up the Mill Hill Mission. They drained their ascetic budget at the only expensive hotel in town, probably the Rajah's Arms, a government attempt at hostelry in the 1870s. The Rajah then permitted them to pitch their tents on a spot south along Rock Road, where the Catholic Mission's head-quarters was erected, and where the St Joseph's Cathedral, a convent, and a chapel were granted some hectares of land. Visitors to Kuching in this period had found a dearth of hotels in the thriving town. Female guests were accommodated at the Astana; official guests stayed at the Residency situated south of an open field, the Central Padang (now the Plaza Merdeka). James Austin Wilder, the American visitor, found that he was putting up at the dingy wooden Rest House, 'where out-station officers stop when they come down river to report'. In the Padang, the Rajah's band of Filipino players from the Sarawak Rangers performed twice a week at the Garden Esplanade, a pavilion-like structure. Wilder was rudely startled when the band—the Rajah's pride—began its performance with a resounding 'crash' at precisely five o'clock in the afternoon.

New rows of shophouses like those on Khoo Hung Yeang Street and Market Street appeared when Sungei Gartak was reclaimed by the early 1880s. The tide-eroded river banks along the Main Bazaar and market places were strengthened with retention walls and piled with *belian* trunks. In 1902, fresh mountain water from a new reservoir at Matang came directly into the town via pipes that ran the marathon along the beds of the Sarawak River at Satok. The Ranee Margaret, who was said to have watched Kuching's growth 'from the verandah of the Astana', recalled that the town at the end of the century was so 'neat and fresh and prosperous …' that it reminded her 'of a box of painted toys kept scrupulously clean by a child'.

## People and Progress

Small groups of Hakkas returned to Kuching to do trading in the 1880s, albeit with a damaged commercial credibility on top of the disparagement by the other dialect groups for their 'coarse' farming background. Yet the government had tremendous admiration for the Hakkas' agricultural energies. In 1898, the Kapitan General Ong Tiang Swee, son of Ong Ewe Hai, was urged to sponsor a hundred Hakka Christians from southern China to Kuching. These were employed to plant padi on a 60-hectare land 4.8 kilometres south on Penrissen Road leading to Serian district. The project fizzled out, but the district grew into a thriving Hakka vegetable farming community. The Rajah then offered free lands specifically for planting gambier and pepper, with free passages on the government steamers, and tax-free export for the first six years. The Kuching *towkay* were urged to join the Borneo Company and to help establish the Sarawak Steamship Company in 1875. The increased steamship services eased Kuching's expanding trade, and facilitated the influx of more Chinese into the country. The capital was now the main port of call, as well as a distributing and administrative centre for immigrant workers and settlers in Sarawak. The majority of Chinese, adherent to dialect group enterprises for the convenience of communication and familiar cultural background, chose to come as free immigrants, or as coolies to Chinese traders. The Rajah permitted the Hokkien and Teochew *towkay* to handle the lucrative coolie trade—buying and selling the coolies off via the boats that arrived with the north-east monsoon at the Main Bazaar wharf. At the end of the century, Kuching had a community of wealthy Hokkien and Teochew merchants with a proliferation of trade networks in outlying districts, and strong economic links to Singapore and Thailand's Chinese commercial worlds.

The Nakhodas began to assimilate with the Malay élite population as the Rajah increasingly encouraged businesses to be done on a large scale. The only foreign competition that the Chinese faced, and vice versa, was the Borneo Company with their similar trading, shipping, and mining ventures. The bustling atmosphere of Market Street and Gambier Road marked the success of the gambier and

1. The *Royalist*, flying the St George, moored on the Sarawak River, in front of James Brooke's first residence on the north bank. (*Illustrated News of the World*, 1858)

2. Audience Hall of Rajah Muda Hassim where James Brooke was first received in 1839. (Antiques of the Orient)

3. James Brooke, the First Rajah. (Sarawak Museum)

4. The Government House was built on the site of The Grove in 1852. This wooden structure was demolished in 1869 to give way to the Astana.

5. India Street (originally Kling Street) is today a pedestrian mall. It features shops owned by Malays, Chinese, and Indians. (Darrell Tsen)

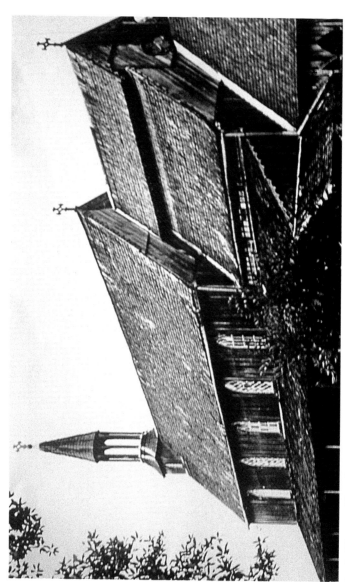

6. St Thomas Church. (Courtesy of the Anglican Diocese of Kuching)

7. Dayak houses at Padungan. (Courtesy of the Anglican Diocese of Kuching)

8. Return of war *prahu* to the Sarawak River at Kuching after a punitive expedition. (Antiques of the Orient)

9. HMS *Samarang* capsized in the middle of the Sarawak River. (Antiques of the Orient)

10. Kuching in 1858, water-colour by Harriette McDougall. (Harriette McDougall, *Letters from Sarawak Addressed to a Child*, London, Grant & Griffiths, 1854)

11. Charles Brooke, the Second Rajah. (Sarawak Museum)

12. The present-day Astana. Built in 1870, the Astana was the first concrete building in Kuching. (Alice Yen Ho)

13. The Satok Suspension Bridge was built in 1926 and formed a link between the north and south banks of the Sarawak River. (Darrell Tsen)

14. The Chinese Court is situated opposite the Tua Pek Kong Temple at the end of the Main Bazaar. It was used as the Chinese Chamber of Commerce after 1920 and is now the Chinese Historical Museum. (Darrell Tsen)

15. The Court House was completed in 1874 and the Charles Brooke Memorial was added in 1924. (Darrell Tsen)

16. The SquareTower, built as a fort and dungeon, was used as a dance hall in the 1920s. (Darrell Tsen)

17. Fort Margherita, named after the Ranee Margaret, was built in 1879. (Alice Yen Ho)

18. The Tua Pek Kong Temple is believed to have begun as a small wooden shrine in the mid-eighteenth century. (Darrell Tsen)

19. The McDougalls' Sandrock Cottage at Santubong. (Courtesy of the Anglican Diocese of Kuching)

pepper trades. In 1899 the government imported 380 Indian labourers, both male and female, from India to ease the shortage of labour. They were given three-year contracts to work in the Rajah's Matang estates, and for the Public Works Department in road construction and engineering projects.

Chinese associations, formed as early as the 1850s to organize trade and maintain temples, operated their Chinese schools in a desultory manner. Due to this, wealthy families sent their children to China or Singapore for Chinese education, or engage private tutors from China to coach their children. The Rajah encouraged Chinese education (in dialects), for he believed that Asian students did not need a Western education which would tend to stuff them 'with a lot of subjects that they do not require to know' (Brooke, 1866). In 1912, the Hokkien Association, under the aegis of the Rajah, opened the Hokkien Free School. In 1916 the Teochew Association started the Min Tek School. However, the presence of the missionary schools for boarding and day students greatly influenced the literacy-conscious Chinese with their regimented English schooling system. St Thomas was particularly popular for its atmosphere of an English public school, and was said to be thought highly of by the government, especially in ensuring employment for its graduates. (This conception bred deep rivalry between St Thomas and St Joseph which lasted till the end of the colonial era.) The predominant students of both schools were the Christian Hakkas, and those from the dominant Hokkien population. Together with the Malay élite and Dayak students, they were to fill the expanding government posts as clerks, boys (peons), typists, and teachers. This was in the 1930s. The Malay schools in Kampong Gersik and Kampong Jawa, and the Government Lay School started by the Rajah in 1902, trained the Malays for clerical positions in the government service. The latter two were merged in 1931 and renamed the Maderasah Melayu (Malay College) in Kampong Jawa, with a curricular emphasis on the Malay language and the Islamic religion. The Malay élite, however, were invariably educated at one of the missionary schools, while the poorer ones often aimed at attending one too instead of the neighbourhood schools.

## Work and Celebration

The Sarawak River remained a major commuting route and a venue for entertainment. For instance, the firing of a gun announcing a steamer from Singapore would draw a large crowd to the wharf. Until the Satok Suspension Bridge was completed in 1926 (see Chapter 6), the north and south banks were not linked (Colour Plate 13). The river was still infested with those 'mischievous alligators', some of which were 5 metres long. In 1878, the *Sarawak Gazette* reported that of the 266 crocodiles caught during the year, 153 were from Sarawak River. The Rajah as the supreme ruler is said to have sentenced such 'murderers' to death.

At the New Year's Day Regatta the whole population would throng the embankment as boat owners competed for trophies . A great variety of racing boats belonging to the *towkay*, the *datu*, and the European officers, displayed their owners' affluence. Punitive expeditions against the insubordinate Dayaks and the Orang Ulu were being gradually replaced with 'peace making' ceremonies in the 1890s. The river now reverberated with the battle din of the Regatta, which was claimed to be a sport that the Englishmen took with them everywhere they went. Kuching's Race Week, held in August, was another town event initiated in 1890. It is said to have been influenced by the Rajah's love for riding, and inspired by his Derbyshire county officers. All officers stationed elsewhere other than the town were obliged to gather in the capital for the special event. Sports events, fund-raising, pony and horse racing, luncheons, dinner balls, and drinking parties were held to encourage 'the mingling of people'. Two days were devoted to races—with ponies from North Borneo (Sabah), and horses from Australia. For the highlight, the whole populace 'swarmed out on foot' to the Race Course at Padungan. There was participation from all. It was like getting every 'Asiatic nationality ... all gay and carefree—out for a holiday' (Archer, 1948).

The arrival of the Indian labourers made possible the paving of more roads that extended right into the suburbs, where the Europeans lived in houses with gardens and English names, and the prosperous Chinese in their mansions. The roads were surfaced with antimony slags—remnants of smelted antimony from the mines—or with coastal shingles. These withstood the heavy rainfalls, and the treading of bullock carts, handcarts with iron wheels, and European horses and gharries (Plate 16). The vehicles to mark Kuching's progress were the Shanghai rickshaws imported from Singapore in 1895. These were originally called the 'jinricksha' in Japanese—culled from the Chinese word *jen-li-che* meaning 'man-powered vehicle'. The roads were filled with coolies (mostly from the Henghua and Hockchia groups) transporting at top speed their prosperous *towkay*, European officers, housewives, and servants with their market loads. Accidents were frequent as Kuching's roads traversed knolls and valleys, and passengers were reportedly tipped out of the post-haste vehicle. At one time, no less than 300 rickshaws lined the busy streets and junctions. The rich would own a private rickshaw complete with a 'chauffeur', and, 'if one was very corpulent … one had both a puller and a pusher'. John Archer, a Brooke officer, reminisced in 1948 that they were 'nice to ride about', better than the jeep (that was to come), and

16. Gharries were used by the Rajah and his officers as well as by the *datu* around Kuching town. (Sarawak Museum)

39

were 'altogether an asset and a delight'. It appeared like an idyllic time when 'rickshas thread their way noiselessly through the animated street, while creaking bullock carts ponderously hold the road' (Ward, 1966).

4

# A Little Model Metropolis

Kuching [in 1899] has many open spaces, public gardens with bright flowers and well-kept laws [sic] ... it is a little model metropolis of a model state.

(Arthur B. Ward, *Rajah's Servant*, 1966)

CAPTAIN Sir Henry Keppel who had visited Kuching in 1867 could hardly recognize the town when he made his last trip to the Far East in 1900. At a banquet in his honour at the Astana he apologized for not dressing formally (in his 'medalled' uniform), for he had imagined that Kuching was still in the jungle. Vast changes had taken place in the thirty years since his last visit. The pace of progress gathered momentum from the early 1900s. Rubber seeds (*Hevea braziliensis*), introduced in Kuching in the 1880s, had become the tree of prosperity, while the price of gambier dropped with the advent of synthetic dyes. A 'rush' for rubber began when the soil around Kuching was found to be most suitable for planting rubber. More Chinese from Singapore and China, Malays from Brunei and other districts and Indonesia, Ibans from the Second and Third Divisions, and some Japanese migrated to the First Division to work in the rubber 'garden', or to own one. Javanese labourers were for the first time contracted to work on the Government and the Borneo Company's rubber estates.

The high revenues and low expenses of the outlying districts had created huge balances by the late 1890s. Kuching's treasury reported solvent figures of 1.7 million dollars in 1917, and 3.44 million in 1923. The First World War did not affect Kuching adversely. Conversely, a greater demand for rubber during the war led to another rubber boom in the region in the 1920s. The 1929 stock market crash, however, halted all rubber industries. The Great Depression of the 1930s was felt in Kuching and districts around, where cash crops had been staked for rubber. Nevertheless, the Chartered Bank, and three Chinese-owned banks were opened in the same period chiefly for trading purposes in Kuching.

In 1911, the Chinese in Kuching celebrated the success of China's Revolution with the ubiquitous firecrackers. While older men hung on to their queues for years, the better-informed generation relinquished theirs with alacrity. The fall of the Manchus gave the Tamil barbers in Kuching an unprecedented 'trimming' business after the 'more crude removal of the *towchang* [pigtail] had been performed'. Shops were permitted to put up their shutters, and 'flags of various colors ... were flying from upper windows, while there was a kind of suppressed excitement in the air, giving the impression that this was not an ordinary festival occasion' (*Sarawak Gazette*, November 1911). In 1912, the establishment of a Chinese court, that convened in a new Chinese Court building on the river bank opposite the Tua Pek Kong temple, marked the rapport between the Brooke government and the increasing Chinese population (Colour Plate 14). Kapitan General Ong Tiang Swee was the spokesperson for all the dialect groups, which were each represented by their own Kapitan (Plate 17). The leaders sat with

17. Ong Tiang Swee, the Kapitan General of Kuching with other Supreme Council members. (Sarawak Museum)

the native officers on the Supreme Council, one of the powerful governing bodies of the Brooke government. Between 1910 and 1930, thousands of Chinese had settled in Kuching. The Indian population saw considerable increase of Tamil Hindus, including professionals like doctors, teachers, and clerks. The Tamils and Sikhs found it expedient to attend the missionary schools. The more conservative Indian Muslim merchants set up their own schools, and taught religious subjects in Arabic.

## From Bullock Carts to Railways

Telecommunications first arrived with the introduction of the telephone in 1906 followed by the telegraph ten years later. In October 1916, test messages from the new wireless station at Rock Road were sent to Singapore and Penang. (In the following May, it promptly relayed the news of the Second Rajah's death in England.) The Kuching government soon tuned in to the radio for news updates of the war. The pragmatic Second Rajah saw the need for Kuching to be ahead with new technologies. He

18. The Sarawak Government Railway ran for 16 kilometres south of Kuching and was closed in 1933. (Sarawak Museum)

43

planned a 38-kilometre railway service for Kuching in 1906. The
Sarawak Government Railway began running in 1915 but only up
to 16 kilometres and with five stations (Plate 18). It consisted of
seven passenger coaches, five open freight wagons, five covered
wagons, and two break vans, with three locomotives named Bulan,
Bintang, and Jean. The railway ran parallel to the old Rock Road
starting from its terminus near the Masjid Besar down to a bazaar in
Serian, with the simple aim of freighting crops and passengers. For
a time it was also used to convey fresh milk from the new dairy
farm in an ice-chilled train car into Kuching. It once ran an evening
service for townfolks to return before nightfall after visiting their
farms, and for rural folks to get home before midnight. The railway
service was closed in 1933 as it incurred a loss of more than a
million dollars. The train fare was expensive compared to the up
and coming bus services that stopped at more stations, or even at
any spot in the suburb that the passengers might wish to alight
(Plate 19).

In Kuching's unique governing system devised by the Second

19. Bus transport in the 1900s. (Sarawak Museum)

Rajah, the Third Rajah ruled in tandem with his brother, Tuan Muda Bertram Brooke, who 'held the fort' in his brother's absence during the summer months. In the peaceful decades of this era, however, the forts in Kuching had in custody the dried skulls confiscated from the Dayak longhouses. The Third Rajah's era saw the only major building, the General Post Office, famed for its Corinthian columns and archways, being constructed in 1931 on the site of the Rajah's stables. The Charles Brooke Memorial, a granite structure that was located in front of the Court House, was erected in 1924 through special funds raised by the public (the balance of the funds went into forming a Leper's Settlement at the 13th Mile named after the Second Rajah).

In 1907 the Borneo Company manager, J. M. Bryan, was the first person in town to own a motor car. This 10–12 hp Coventry Humber was a sensation in Kuching. Following closely was the first motor cycle that the then Rajah Muda Vyner rode into town, much to the abhorrence of the old Rajah. The prosperous Malay *datu* were among the first people to own motor cars. The rickshaws began to phase out in the motoring age. The Henghua and Hockchia people, like their counterparts in the Malayan states, progressed from 'kan-chia'—literally 'pulling the vehicle' in Hokkien—to the car tyre and bicycle businesses. They also mastered driving skills and operated taxis. The rickshaws remained a swift town facility, with some surviving well into the 1950s (Plate 20).

In 1870, Marianne North, a visiting American artist remarked that Kuching looked magical from the Astana in the evening. The town glittered with street lights from oil lamps in the pitch dark. In 1906, the iron posts of the new street lights on which gas lamps were mounted elicited much pride from the people. The new lighting system had made a metropolis of the kampong town. The only hitch was that the lights went out easily 'because the Swedish producers of the incandescent petroleum gas had not counted on the vagaries of Kuching weather'. The people in Kuching were nevertheless pleased; now they 'could lift their heads high', and no longer needed to suffer 'the taunts of the people of Singapore who had had street-lighting for thirty years' (Payne, 1966). Electric street

20. A rickshaw that survived into the 1950s in Kuching. (Sarawak Museum)

lighting followed in 1923, another twenty years after Singapore first started using it.

### Famous but Unknown

Sir James Brooke was a legend in Singapore's mercantile world for making Borneo's coasts safe for trade, complementing his idol Sir Stamford Raffles' eradication of piracy in the Straits Settlements. The *Singapore Free Press* had reported the progress of Sarawak under its First Rajah. Naturalists, anthropologists, and archaeologists had explored and published books and essays on its primeval jungle and its Dayak people. The well-known naturalist and co-author of the Darwinian theory, Alfred Russel Wallace (1823–1913), wrote part of his papers in Santubong while visiting Kuching between 1854 and 1856. During Charles Brooke's reign, Kuching was a booming capital town that imported coolies from Singapore, China, and

India, with a weekly steamer servicing between Singapore and Kuching. Tobacco from the Rajah's Matang estates was exported to England, and Matang tea and coffee were drunk in the European social circles of Penang in the late nineteenth century.

Yet, beyond its shores, Kuching remained relatively unknown in the late 1890s. Wilder first visited Johor Bahru in 1896, and found that '... nobody knows anything about Borneo here. The ignorance is awful.' Earlier in 1878, Hornaday had expressed similar sentiments, as had Ward in 1899. Colonial observers alleged that the *Singapore Free Press* did not bother to send reporters to Kuching, while the capital seemed unwelcoming as reflected in its inadequate accommodation facilities.

With the dawn of the 1920s, the world became aware of the old capital of Sarawak. In 1922 Sarawak (indicating Kuching) was said to be 'making a striking show' at the British Empire Exhibition in Wembley, London. Among the shows of forestry (wood and parquet), agriculture, and native arts and crafts, was 'an array of cannon captured from pirates by former rajahs at one time or another, and judging by the appearance of the firearms, the pirates must have obtained them either by fair or foul means from the European adventurers in the old days' (*Sarawak Gazette*, May 1922). In the 1924 Exhibition, Kuching was represented by miniatures of the 'Astana Tower' and the 'Colonnade' (Court House). The world was reminded once again that Borneo was a land of headhunters when Singapore males were rumoured to be averse to marrying Kuching girls for fear that they might have Dayak 'blood', and hence the base instinct to take heads, perhaps doing it in the middle of the night.

In 1920, Joseph Conrad wrote to the Ranee Margaret in England, confiding in her that his novel *Lord Jim* was 'inspired in great measure by the history of the first Rajah's enterprise.... Even the very name of the messenger [Japar] ... was taken from that source' (Payne, 1966). (Japar was the slave who brought the ring that James Brooke gave Badruddin, with the tragic news of the murder of Badruddin and Muda Hassim in Brunei in 1846.) Somerset Maugham visited Kuching and other districts in 1921, and wrote his famous collection of Borneo short stories. In the 1930s, the Ranee Sylvia toured Europe and America and lived a high society life with her two younger daughters, whom the fashionable afternoon newspapers had honoured with the title 'princesses'. Rajah Vyner had frowned on this; in his own words, he would not have all that 'high falutting'. The Third Rajah was an excruciatingly shy man who hated publicity, while Sylvia 'exploited to the utmost her exotic role as the "Ranee of Sarawak"' (Reece, 1993). Following Sylvia and her daughters' dabbling in films, a team of Hollywood producers flew into town in their seaplanes in 1932 to consider making a movie of Kuching with Errol Flynn playing the role of Rajah James Brooke.

By the 1910s, movies had become popular among the people in Kuching. One silent-movie cinema operated in a stuffy Carpenter Street shop premise, where the female audience were strictly seated away at the balcony on the upper floor. Another cinema at Khoo Hung Yeang Street was called the Globe Theatre. Vyner Brooke built the Sylvia in 1934, which showed the latest Western films. The Ranee Sylvia said it was 'the finest cinema in the East, and even in Singapore they are forced to admit it is superior'. In the Malay kampongs, the *gendang Melayu* was an old popular socio-cultural entertainment. The evening's activities included feasting and dancing. Young '*gendang* girls' recited *pantuns* (poetry) accompanied by the mesmerizing beats of their drums, while young men proved their equal with witty repartees. The Third Rajah was known to have held *gendang* competitions at the Astana. In the cinemas, Bangsawan troupes with Indonesian, Malayan, and Singapore artistes made regular live appearances, attracting the whole cosmopolitan population.

## A Centenary Town

Kuching's bazaar was a gravitating centre of both the pressing daily lives of work and businesses, and the social night life of food and entertainment. By the late 1920s, it had become a full-fledged Chinese area. In 1919, the *Sarawak Gazette* had reported on the overcrowding of businesses in the town core; yet new shops continued to emerge. The housing accommodation was 'nothing short of disgraceful'. In 1924 there were 'waifs and strays' in the bazaar, and vagrants were sleeping and begging in the streets. Meanwhile, some two hundred shops were opened at Padungan district. The post-sago industrial area was fast becoming a new centre of commercial activities commensurate with those of the old town. The old bazaars, relieved of congestion, were characterized by their traditional variety of trades, and by the government offices and official activities. The Main Bazaar maintained its major commercial activities run by Hokkien and Chao Ann entrepreneurs. Both Carpenter and Upper China Streets were concentrated with Hakka and Cantonese artisan trades. India Street thrived with textile shops of Indian and European goods. General trading in Khoo Hung Yeang Street soon gave way to the reputation of being the 'red light district' housing Japanese brothels with women from Japan or Singapore. Gambier Road of the post-gambier economy became a centre of Teochew grocery, rubber, and market trades.

The air services developed after the capital saw its first seaplanes in 1924. The HMS *Pegasus*, enroute from Singapore to Miri, deployed three seaplanes to Kuching on the day the Charles Brooke Memorial at the Court House was being unveiled in a solemn ceremony. The seaplanes flew over the town for a brief show of 'air ballet' and landed on the river in front of the Main Bazaar. The Royal Air Force made subsequent visits to Kuching, landing at the waters off Pending Wharf, about 1.6 kilometres east of the town. In 1934 the 1 September issue of the *Singapore Free Press* was sent by airmail to Kuching on the same day that it was published. This issue carried an announcement on the event. By 1937, Kuching had an airfield built at 7th Mile; it was 650 metres long and 270 metres wide. Four years later it was quickly destroyed in the face of imminent advances of the Japanese army.

In 1941, with the sound of war in the air, food defences were built up, especially the storage of padi. Girls of marriageable age were matched off, and young men married early to shun conscription. The first detachment of the Indian Punjabi Battalion arrived in April in the new Batu Lintang barracks 5 kilometres south of the town. Kuching, now a century old, had hitherto celebrated its 'national' day on 24 September with great fanfare and holidays. A significant event in this jubilant centenary celebration, however, was the proclamation of the new Constitution by the Third Rajah, by which more self-government was granted to the Sarawak people. The Rajah was no longer the absolute ruler.

The war arrived on 19 December 1941, and Kuching ceased being the capital of an independent sovereign state.

# 5
# The Pioneering Communities

The inhabitants may be divided into three different classes, viz. the Malays, the Chinese, and the Dyaks; of the two former little need be said, as they are so well known.

(James Brooke's Journal, 1841)

IN the 1850s it was not uncommon to find Dayak warriors, garbed only in bright red or white loin cloth, and 'bristling with swords and spears, with tigers' teeth inserted in the upper part of their ears, and huge black and white hornbill feathers rising from their heads', strolling the streets of Kuching (Payne, 1966). James Brooke had 'insisted' on the presence of Dayaks in the town, the early Balau community in the bazaar being an example. His Government House was always filled with native officers consulting with him, and with Iban and Land Dayaks quietly making petitions or seeking the Rajah's advice. The Second Rajah did not favour the Dayaks dwelling in town. In the November 1902 issue, a column in the *Sarawak Gazette* lamented that the Dayaks living in the Kuching vicinity, hanging around the government offices and European houses, seemed to have lost the pride they and their ancestors once possessed. Despite this gloomy view, Ibans from the Second and Third Divisions continued to immigrate to Kuching in the early 1900s when the rubber economy was at its peak. These Ibans influenced the Kuching Ibans to a great extent. In the 1930s, the urban Ibans formed co-operatives, and, as the Chinese and the Nakodas had done, owned boats and traded goods with river settlements. Despite Charles Brooke's arduous attempt at keeping them from the 'corruption of Western civilization', and the Third Rajah's preference for Malay civil services, many Ibans were graduating from missionary schools in the 1930s. Their *berjalai* tradition had evolved into leaving their homes for overseas education or urban working experiences. They were employed mainly in military forces, 'out-station' government posts, and in the Sarawak Museum. The Land Dayaks had preferred to dwell in the suburb, and only took up occasional work in town. The 1950s saw a gradual influx of different groups of Dayak into Kuching, a move that was encouraged by the colonial government.

## The Chinese

Harriette McDougall noticed that Kuching's Chinese 'were not all of the same tribe, and could not understand one another'. The Kuching Chinese communities comprised at least three major and three minor dialect groups, each with its sub-dialect division. An illustration can be drawn from the anecdote of the Second Rajah riding into the country one morning when he came upon a Chinese woman breaking the ground in her vegetable garden. On returning later he found that the garden had been meticulously laid out. Upon being told that the woman was a Sin-ann Hakka, the Rajah was keen to send for more of the same people, particularly the men, whom he thought would double the women in diligence and strength. Little did the Rajah realize that among the Sin-ann Hakka, the women were the working force in the fields while their men were largely 'homemakers'. (The migrant Hakkas never had the feet-binding tradition.) Charles Brooke did pass through 'Chinese gardens spreading over many hundreds of acres', and had marvelled at the farmers' 'wonderful knack of making the most of a bit of ground'. He was, however, unimpressed at their sloppy jobs in building houses where their eyes seemed to be 'extremely crooked' (C. Brooke, 1866).

The Chinese in Nanyang came from the southern Chinese provinces of Fujian, Guangdong, Guangxi, and Hainan Island. A small number came from central China like Jiangxi, Hupeh, or Shanghai. Many like Ong Ewe Hai had left Singapore to trade or extend families (Plate 21). Each group came with their own culture, customs, dialects, and their particular trade. They had to adapt to living together among themselves as well as among other nationalities, more so in Sarawak's multi-racial population.

21. Ong Ewe Hai, one of the earliest Hokkien entrepreneurs from Singapore who established his business in Kuching. (Sarawak Museum)

The Hokkiens originated from Fujian, particularly from Quangzhou and Amoy, the seaports famous for their dynamic maritime merchants who had traded overseas since the eighth century. (The Hokkiens of Singapore were Raffles' 'respectable Amoy merchants'.) The Teochews came from the Swatow seaport in Zhaozhou district in south-east Guangdong. They speak a dialect akin to the Hokkien, but has a lilting and lyrical intonation. Kuching's Hokkien dialect has a discernible 'Kuching accent', probably attributable to influences from the local polyglot popula-tion. The Hokkien sub-group, Chao Ann, from Chao Ann district close to the Zhaozhou border, speak their Hokkien with the lilting Teochew intonation. A contemporary of Ong Ewe Hai and Lau Kian Huat, and perhaps even more successful and wealthy, was a Chao Ann man named Chan Koh. He arrived in a Chinese salt merchant's junk in the 1830s and went to Bau to work as a labourer. His rags-to-riches story began when he found traces of gold in his garden soil. Henceforth, Hakka goldminers in Bau were known to have pledged to their deities that should they find gold they would give Chan Koh a share. It was through various small trades that Chan established the well-known Chin Ann Company. He brought more Chao Ann people into Kuching and formed the Chao Ann Association.

'Hakka' in Cantonese, and 'Kheh' in Hokkien (from 'Ke-Jia' in Mandarin), both refer to the 'guest people'. They were originally northern Chinese who had migrated centuries ago into all parts of China, and dwelt as 'guests' to the locals. The Hakkas in Nanyang came mainly from the hilly northern Guangdong areas. 'Cantonese' is a Western term for the Guangzhou people from the Pearl Delta region of Guangdong. The early Hainanese (or Hylam) from Hainan were chiefly cooks or houseboys to European officers, and later specialized in European cold-storage supplies and coffee shop trade. The Henghua fishermen and Hockchia rickshaw pullers came from the rural hinterland of Fuzhou (the capital of Fujian province). The Foochows from urban Fuzhou came to Kuching in the late 1880s (as distinct from those who came to Sibu in 1901). They were mainly barbers, coffee shop owners, and contractors. Being a more aggressive group, the

22. A hawker with a Chinese government clerk. (Sarawak Museum)

Foochows were to dominate other trades when more of them immigrated to Kuching after the 1940s.

Before the 1950s, Chinese clannish antagonism had discouraged intermarriages among the dialect groups. The wealthy *towkay* would go to Singapore or China to find a compatible wife with similar dialect and family background, as Ong Tiang Swee had done. Before 1900, only a few elderly women with bound feet were seen in public in Kuching. Harriette McDougall wrote that Sing Sing, the Mission's Chinese interpreter, 'put his wife into a large chest with air-holes at the top, and brought her safely from China'. Besides, with Chinese preference for males, baby girls were given to the Malays who brought them up as fair maidens.

The missionary-educated Kuching-born Chinese emerged in the 1930s as a new generation that spoke Hokkien and English. Rather than going into trades, these took up all levels of government service and clerical positions in the Borneo Company (Plate 22). These 'Sarawak Chinese' were equivalent to the Straits-born Chinese who identified themselves as Peranakan (though without intermarriage with Malays as in the true Peranakan) (Lockard, 1987). Contemporaneous to the Straits-born Chinese women of non-Peranakan descent, Kuching-born Chinese women, from rich business families and who were English educated, started to wear the Malay sarong and kebaya. They were greeted as *nonya*, and were regarded as *baba* or Peranakan acculturated. These Sarawak Chinese were westernized to a certain degree through western education and, apart from speaking Hokkien, were vaguely acquainted with Chinese culture (unlike the Chinese educated, or the bilingual). Many post-colonial Sarawak Chinese have used only forks and spoons from their grandparents' days (Third Rajah era). Many are only learning to use the chopsticks and Mandarin as a result of being exposed to the business world.

## The Malays

Sarawak has its version of a popular legend about the origin of the Malay élite in Borneo. The Datu Merpati, a Javanese prince, married the Datu Permaisuri, eldest daughter of Raja Jarom of Johore from the royal house of Minangkabau. They settled near Santubong. Their son, Merpati Jepang, married Dayang Murdiah, daughter of the Santubong chief, and they moved to live in Lidah Tanah. The Kuching *datu* had claimed lineage from Merpati Jepang's regal genealogy. In general, the Sarawak Malays in Kuching are an integration of a number of races in the region—Nakhodas (with Minangkabau origins), Sumatrans, Javanese, Bugis, Arab Sharifs, Brunei Pengirans, Indian Muslims, the local Melanau, Land Dayak, Kedayan tribes, and the Chinese through adoption. (Like the Dayak's *berjalai*, the Minangkabaus have their *merantau* or 'wandering' tradition—young men leaving the villages in Sumatra, and sojourning elsewhere, sometimes never to return.)

At the pinnacle of the early Malay élite class were the Datu Patinggi (Supreme Chief), the Datu Bandar (Port Chief), and the Datu Temenggong (Commander-in-Chief). The top positions of the native officer throughout the Brooke eras had remained with the family and descendants of Datu Patinggi Ali (who died in 1844). The *datu*'s hegemony in the government services diminished towards the post-colonial period. Present-day Kuching Malays of aristocratic lineage retain their titles in name as signs of respect

56

rather than class. The *datu*'s male descendants are named 'Abang', and the females 'Dayang'. The 'Bangsa Pengiran' marks the kin of former Brunei Pengirans (like the surviving families of Muda Hassim brought into Kuching by James Brooke) but is not frequently used. Those of Arab ancestry claiming descent from the Prophet Mohammad are called Sharif, and Tuanku (My Master), and Wan, if it is before marriage. The females are named Sharifas, who in the past never married a non-Sharif.

A Minangkabau immigrant group that the *datu* highly respected and permitted to marry into the *perabangan* class consisted of the wealthy and intellectual religious teachers. The early prestigious Minangkabau immigrants had maintained their status with their Sumatran style of dress and speech, and kept to their Kampong Gersik. The characteristic warmth of the Malays in Kuching, with the unambiguous authority of the *datu*, and the stable Brooke government, was gradually passed on to these immigrants. Their assimilation into the Malay community brought about a distinguished class of civil servants, religious teachers, and leaders. Two notable teachers were Encik Ahmad Shawal Abdul Hamid, and Encik Abu Bakar. The latter was to become the Ranee Margaret's Malay language teacher.

The *datu*, the religious teachers, and a small number of Peranakan Jawi—civil servants and teachers of Indian Muslim and Malay mixed descent brought in by James Brooke from Penang and Singapore—formed the upper echelon of the early Malay society. The Boyanese grooms, Javanese contract labourers, local Malay peasants, fishermen, and freed slaves from the élite households in 1886 constituted the large sector of the 'unlettered' *Orang Pereman*, or Free Citizens. The *datu* of the Brooke era lived an almost European lifestyle in Kampong Datu (Plate 23). They had large houses with stables of ponies and carriages, and later motor cars. They owned horses that raced at Race Week, and boats that competed at the Regatta. The aristocratic Malay women were veiled from gazes with the 'Sarawak veil', an extension of the sarong that wraps around the head (almost like a sari) (Plate 24). Women of the *pereman* class were distinguished by their mandatory

23. A group of Malay *datu*, *c.*1918. (Sarawak Museum)

24. The Ranee Margaret wearing the Malay costume with Malay aristocratic ladies. (Sarawak Museum)

unveiled head and bare feet. When these non-élite people walked past the *datu's* houses they had to lower their umbrellas, even if no one was at home to accept the expression of respect.

The 1920s saw the emergence of the *Orang Kerani* (clerks). This was an English-educated Malay 'middle class' who spoke English, and ate with forks and spoons when in public. The new group had developed from the lower echelon aristocrats and the increasing number of *Orang Pereman*. They made up the Malay civil service, a group with much prestige attached and given opportunities to wealth and security similar to those of the vanished Nakhodas.

## The Indians

The Brooke regime had regarded the Malay native officers as 'gentlemen who should not soil their hands at trade'. The Chinese formed the economic backbone, while the Ibans excelled militarily with their traditional prowess at survival in the harsh jungles. It was the small Indian community that was ultimately to make up the third group of Kuching's pioneers. Before the 1940s the Indians in the region were a large transient group of men who led a frugal peaceful life wherever they settled to trade. The Moplah Muslim traders were able to integrate freely with the Malays through a cohesive religion, and a familiar Hindu base in the Malay cultural and social life (Plate 25). Most Indian men went home to get married, then sojourned singly, and visited their families every few years. Only a small percentage of Chinese immigrants realized their dream of retiring in China, but most Indians achieved their goal of returning to live in India. This was one of the reasons the Indians remained a minority group in any settlement, with no exception in Kuching.

In the 1860s, the Sepoys, consisting of Punjabi Sikhs and Bengali Hindus, were the first Northern Indians to come to Kuching. The Sikhs were reputed for enforcing law and order, and were subsequently the Brooke officers' favourite recruits from India or Singapore. This minority Indian group was distinctive in their stalwart appearance, for which they were often engaged, at retirement, as *jagas*, or security guards in banks, godowns, Borneo

25. Two Indian Moplah merchants, Mastan and K. Medin, and a Malay, Abdullah, with the Chinese Teochew towkay, Lau Kian Huat. (Sarawak Museum)

Company stores, and cinemas. Being versatile and pragmatic, they soon branched out into diverse businesses, and were renowned for their real estate and money-lending enterprises. The younger generations formed a part of the Kuching mission-school students who, since the 1930s, have graduated into more professional fields.

In the 1860s, southern Indian Tamil Hindus immigrated freely into Kuching where they were employed by Europeans to work on their new estates and plantations, and in their households and gardens. The larger group of Tamil labourers imported under government contract in the 1890s were from Madras, Sri Lanka, and Kerala. When the Matang estates closed in 1912, many had opted to go back to India. Some of these later applied to the Rajah to return as they missed their 'home' in Kuching. The Tamil labourers in the construction fields were the Indian pioneers who built Kuching's infrastructure, especially in laying roads like the Penrissen, the 7th Mile Airport Road, the railway tracks, and worked in the major building and engineering projects in town.

Much like all Indian communities in the region, the various

groups of the early Indians in Kuching maintained their own identity in food, culture, customs, festivities, and especially in their religions and languages. Among the English-speaking Indian professionals was a prominent Tamil, K. V. Krishna, who, in the 1920s, led the Indian groups in a social awareness movement to improve the image of the Kuching Indian communities. This was similar to the tide of Malay and Chinese ethnic consciousness in the same period. The Indian Association was formed in 1938 to co-ordinate the various groups, but Kuching's Indians remain a minority group with their multi-faceted cultures.

Although post-colonial development brought a greater diversification of races and other Malaysians to Kuching, it is still a predominantly Chinese and Malay town. The small number of Eurasians, that is, those with a European father and a Chinese or Dayak mother, were affiliated to either the Chinese or the Dayak community. Early Japanese sojourners and rubber planters in the pre-occupation years were deported along with the remaining Japanese soldiers after the liberation.

The early residential pattern of Chinese, Malay, and Indian 'kampongs' in the town seemed to give old Kuching an element of population segregation. Yet the people have had a long history of close-knit cohabitation. Besides major annual events, ceremonies or government functions, each race has had interest in the other's cultural festivities and way of life. People of all races would curiously pack performances such as the temple *wayang* (opera), Malay *bangsawan*, and Chinese or Indian temple processions. The cinemas and the Chinese coffee shops too were popular haunts for all races and creeds, who seemed to be familiar with, and enjoyed, rather than patronized, movies pertaining to the various language, racial, and ethnic groups. This cohesiveness created a people whose somewhat metropolitan image has been a source of their pride and sophistication. Following the colonial period, the increased population spread out into new residential estates that saw a random admixture of people. The present city's two municipal councils are led by a Malay and a Chinese mayor respectively. Each has jurisdiction over their respective districts as well as the larger suburban areas with Malay, Chinese, Dayak, or Indian neighbourhoods.

# 6
# Landmarks and Legends

It is common among the Eastern races that a legend passed down
from father to son for many generations eventually attains the
dignity of a fact and is accepted by all.

(W. J. Chater, *Sarawak Long Ago*, 1969)

ONE legend has it that the Santubong Mountain was thrust up
from the ocean by a volcanic upheaval millions of years ago. In the
process its molten gold spewed out and was spread thinly throughout the district, so that no concentrated gold deposits were ever
found in one location in the First Division. During the stormy
Landas season, fishermen at the foothills made a living panning
for gold in the sandy reefs and streams. The Chinese returning
to China in the 1850s spoke of how Chan Koh found gold in his
garden; Sarawak in Nanyang was a land of gold and opportunities.
It is conjectured by some that the ancient European geographers'
cognizance of the Golden Khersonese in the Malayan region might
have indicated the early Sarawak district. Another geological
feature gave Kuching's surrounding districts certain 'growing rocks'.
These sandstone outcrops would continue to 'exude' after those
that have surfaced have been removed. The early Malays believed
them to be *kramat* or sacred. Rock Road was named after one
such large horizontal brownish outcrop that was found about
3 kilometres south of town. The European officers often used it as
a milestone when exercising their horses. The Second Rajah had
once planned to blast it up to make roads when, ominously,
Kuching had a cholera epidemic, and the Malays 'pleaded success-
fully with him to change his mind'. Hence, the rock still remains.

## *Special Landmarks*

It was likely that Charles Brooke had demolished the Government House in 1869 as it had been associated with some family tragedy. The house had witnessed the unfortunate Johnson Brooke's (1821–68) loss of his two wives and his infant son in the early 1860s. Charles Brooke then built the Astana with the intention of making it his home where he would raise a family. But only the Tuan Muda Bertram was born there in 1876. The original structure of the Astana consisted of three houses, with an official reception room, dining room, and drawing room in the centre portion, and the living quarters in the two adjacent buildings. To keep the guests cool at state dinners or banquets, he would employ the Sarawak Rangers as *punkah wallahs*. At each corner of the table a ranger would swing the Egyptian *punkah*, a large palm frond fan. (An Indian *punkah* would be a large fan suspended from the ceiling.) A feature that was retained from James Brooke's Government House was the entrance hallway, a neo-Gothic castellated tower with the Brooke family crest carved on its wall. Arthur Ward described it as 'a bit of feudal England pitchforked into an Asiatic setting'.

In the Astana backyard, amongst a few graves of the former Brunei prince's family, stands a memorial to the Ranee Margaret's first three children who died at the Red Sea while sailing home to England in 1873. Between the Astana and Fort Margherita is a small fenced-in plot where Johnson Brooke's family had been buried. On the same ground the Malay *datu* had helped to bury the Ranee Margaret's still-born baby when Bishop Chambers refused its burial in the consecrated ground.

A broad open veranda was later added to the front portion of the Astana where the Ranee Margaret often sat and watched Kuching's lively bazaars and river. (It is now closed.) Much to the dismay of the officers at the Court House, the same veranda was the Second Rajah's 'watch tower' from which he took in a complete binocular view of their punctuality at getting into their offices.

In 1858, Charles Brooke in his role as Tuan Muda had demolished and replaced James Brooke's school-house 'Court Room', where Liew Shanbang was alleged to have sat as the 'Chinese Rajah' for two days in 1857. Since its completion in 1874 the new Court House, besides its daily office routines, had been like a town-hall where proclamations and edicts were read, secret society trials were held, and Regatta breakfasts and Race Week luncheons were taken (Colour Plate 15).

The Square Tower (1879) (Colour Plate 16) and the Round Tower (1886) behind the Court House were partially fortified against any sudden attack from the enemy. However, their impregnability, and that of the Fort Magherita, was never proven. The Square Tower, with a medieval dungeon for hard-core prisoners, once functioned as a dance hall in the 1920s. The site of Fort Margherita was chosen for its strategic position; from there the army had a long-distance view downriver to espy approaching enemy boats and *prahu* (Colour Plate 17). From the 1880s, ships steaming upriver would first notice the white Margherita with the Sarawak flag fluttering in the wind. Since 1879 the execution of criminals had been moved from Rock Road to the yard of the fort. The Japanese prisoners of war were also executed there, and this explains why Kuching's inhabitants believe that the surrounding woods are thickly populated by spirits.

Alfred Russel Wallace's visit had planted the seed of the naturalist's interest in Kuching. In 1878, the Second Rajah, with his French valet's assistance, planned for a museum to house the increasing collections of natural species from all over Sarawak. Completed in 1891, the Sarawak Museum was described by some as looking like a 'Normandy town hall', an allusion to the Second Rajah's great interest in French culture (Plate 26). The *Sarawak Gazette* reported in 1925 that in thirty-four years the Museum had had more than 1.5 million visitors. In the 1930s, besides the Museum, visitors would view or cross the Satok Suspension Bridge to get to the north bank. When Charles Brooke in 1902 could not convince his engineer that heaping rocks in the middle of the river would hold up the suspension bridge, the plan was shelved. When the bridge was finally under construction in the 1920s, rumours had it that heads were needed to appease the spirits who lived under the bridge. This was a vestige of the custom of burying a

26. The Sarawak Museum in the early 1900s. (Sarawak Museum)

slave with a longhouse or a bridge construction before slavery was abolished. The rumours died down when a labourer, by coincidence, drowned in the river. In 1926 the bridge lifted the water pipes from the river bed, and joined the two banks. The age of the motor vehicles had arrived in Kuching.

## Religious Establishments

Kuching's oldest and most historical buildings include the various religious establishments. The increase in Malay population in the 1840s and 1850s, particularly with the pious Minangkabau immigrants, seemed to have exerted great influences. Increasingly, the Kuching Malays were joining thousands in Singapore for the Haj to Mecca. The Masjid thrived under a succession of *imams* or religious leaders, and had varied styles in structure over the decades. Its present Moorish style sits majestic as the Masjid Negri (State Mosque) on the same hill overlooking the town core, with gleaming golden cupolas and minarets that are visible from up and downriver. In contrast, the Moplahs' low-roofed Masjid India is sandwiched unobtrusively between India Street and Gambier Road. It is accessible to the informed through a narrow lane from both streets. The Indian merchant community had purchased this original site of their old prayer hut from the Second Rajah. Along Mosque Road and a short distance from the Masjid Negri stands the Sikh Temple. Indian Sepoys who worked in the first barracks near Sungei Gartak were worshipping on the veranda when the Second Rajah came on inspection. He immediately granted them a site nearby to build a temple.

On the southern end of the town are the Anglican and Roman Catholic cathedrals. The original wooden churches, built in the European neo-Gothic style, had been replaced with modern architecture designed to suit the local climate. The Roman Catholic church (1891), a timber and brick structure with two square steeples 24 metres high was replaced in 1968. The Mission House and St Thomas Cathedral were planned by Bishop McDougall, and built by his German carpenter in 1849. The cathedral was rebuilt in 1956. The Mission House is the only surviving wooden building that has withstood time and weather since James Brooke's era, although renovation had been made time and again.

Among the early burials in the Mission House's cemetery were the McDougalls' first three infants who died between 1848 and 1851. A memorial stone also commemorates James Fox and Henry Steele, Brooke officers murdered by the Dayaks in a Third Division fort in 1860. Other graves were those of Alan Lee (1853) and William Brereton (1854). They marked the tough defiance of Rentap and his followers against the Brooke regime, when Lee was killed by Rentap's army in the Batang Lupar skirmish. Following his victory, Rentap, in the tradition of an Iban warrior, composed his own praise-name. A part of it runs as follows:

Earth tremor, land tremor
(*Rentap tanah, Rentap menoa*)
Tuan Lee, easily killed
Tuan Brereton wears women's clothing
And no longer dares to lead the Rajah's forces.

(Pringle, 1970)

At the east end of the town stands Kuching's main Chinese temple, the Tua Pek Kong Temple that started off as a small wooden shrine located just below Bukit Mata Kuching (Colour Plate 18). A legend tells of the deity's complaint through a temple medium in 1965, that its *fengshui* was marred by the iron structure bearing the year '1912' on the roof of the Chinese Court (now Chinese Historical Building) across the street. The structure was removed accordingly. There is a notion that this temple had existed from the 1750s, which tentatively stretches the presence of Kuching's Chinese further back. Its deity, Tua Pek Kong (in Hokkien)—literally translated as 'Big Grand Uncle'—is worshipped by all dialect groups. Any leading pioneer of a settlement can be deified as a Tua Pek Kong after his death so that he would continue to provide blessings to the community. (An example is Liew Shanbang who is worshipped by the Bau Hakkas.) Kuching's Tua Pek Kong is a deified lord of the Zhou Dynasty (1122–255 BC) of China. The Taoist temple at the junction of Wayang and Ewe Hai Streets was built in 1897 in honour of the young Hokkien child deity, Kuek Seng Ong. Allegedly, his image had appeared on some rooftops during Kuching's Great Fire in 1884, waving a black flag just before the rain began to put out the fire. At the same time the Teochew community built their Taoist temple on Carpenter Street to worship Xian Tien Shan Ti or God of Heaven. Both temples nestle close to the missionary ground.

The Hindus had more recent temples built in Kuching. Srinivasagar Kaliamman Temple on Ban Hock Road houses three deities: Lord Subramaniam, Lord Perumal, and the goddess Kaliamman. The statues had come from India with the contracted Tamil workers and were brought to Kuching after the closure of the Matang estates. Another major Hindu goddess, Sri Maha Mariamman, was similarly relocated from the tea estate and worshipped in a nondescript shed for many years at Batu Lintang. Its temple now sits close by the large sacred rock on Rock Road.

## The Resthouses

Early European residents in Kuching often had to contend with the humid climate, beat work stress, and fight diseases such as fever and smallpox. Consequently, they had built some country cottages for quick getaways. The McDougalls' Sandrock Cottage at Santubong had given them brief moments of tranquility and fresh sea breeze (Colour Plate 19). Charles Brooke had a private cottage, the Valambrosa, on his Matang tea estate. These frail structures have long since gone into ruins.

Perhaps the most historical site since the founding of Kuching is in the Serambau foothills where James Brooke put down the rebellion at Fort Belidah in 1841. At about 270 metres on the steep elevation of the Serambau the First Rajah had built, in 1850, a cottage with posts made of *belian* wood. He called it 'Peninjau'— 'Look-afar'. (It has gone into complete ruin). This was but 'a rude wooden lodge where the English Rajah was accustomed to go for relaxation and cool fresh air' (Wallace, 1869). It offered a breath-taking view of the expanse of green jungles and 'silver' rivers in the north, east, and west directions from a landing below the cottage. It was probably during a stay at Peninjau with the Rajah and Spencer St John that Wallace thoroughly confounded James Brooke with the theory of man's evolution from the orang utan. Perhaps too, he was inspired here to name the biggest and most brilliantly coloured butterfly in Sarawak the 'Rajah Brooke' (*Ornithoptera Brookeana*).

A short distance from this area, somewhere near Jugan Siniawan, Liew Shanbang was killed and buried. The tomb is marked by his shrine beside it. Long after the Brookes had left Kuching, these two historical sites are the other reminders to the early making of the old capital.

# 7

# A Romantic Past, A Bustling Present

THE events that took place during the Japanese Occupation in Kuching were numerous, and it would only be fair to have them retold in a separate volume. To attempt to contain them within these pages would do such a historic period grave injustice. Here, it should suffice to say that the Japanese War inflicted little damage on the town's structure. The Allied Forces liberated Kuching in September 1945, and brought it to the turning point of its history. The Third Rajah returned from Australia from where he had been administering his country during the war, and proposed to cede Sarawak to Great Britain as a crown colony. The decision created great uncertainty among the people. For months Kuching was the centre of the cession issue as pro- and anti-cessionists took to the streets. The division cut across races, classes, families, kin, and friends, with the Malays being the most divided. Part of Kuching's people had expected the Rajah Muda Anthony Brooke, Bertram's son, to succeed as the Fourth Rajah. Vyner Brooke (Plate 27), who had no male heir, determined otherwise; the cession was soon over by July 1946.

The colonial government deviated little from the Brooke policies although it put a different stamp over the old capital. A great influx of British officers and Europeans filled up the Kuching administrative posts, and European firms from Singapore and Malaya entered Kuching's market freely. In commerce, the Hokkiens and Chao Anns retained their hegemony. However, a great number of other Chinese dialect groups and Dayak population poured into the First Division. By the 1970s, the Hakkas had replaced the Hokkien majority in Kuching's Chinese population. But Hokkien remains the patois.

Kuching was declared a city in August 1988 with a population of almost 300,000 people. Flyovers are becoming a necessary

27. The Third Rajah, Sir Charles Vyner
Brooke. (Sarawak Museum)

feature of the highways. Traffic thunders over the Sarawak River
on the more solid Tun Haji Abdul Rahman Yakub Bridge after the
Satok Suspension Bridge became a historical monument in the
1970s. Northwards, the highways reach out into the Santubong

villages and coastal resorts, once only accessible by boats and government launches; westwards they stretch into the Matang range. On the south bank, suburban complexes and housing estates are mapped on zones that pepper and rubber gardens once claimed as home.

Yet the idyllic past lingers in the brisk air of the little city. The Astana is now the residence of the Head of State (Governor). From a substantial height on the north bank, the ministerial and administrative buildings fetch a vantage view of the whole city with its modest skyscrapers and rich green foliage. The old kampongs Gersik, Surabaya, and Boyan of the 1840s are still perched on the edge of the river bank while sleek, multi-million ringgit condominiums and shopping complexes loom majestic over them from across the river. Carpenter Street and its lanes stand ambivalent between the centuries: old tea merchants, tailors, smitheries, and coffee shops stay in business amongst electrical appliance and furniture businesses. Antiquity reigns in the quaint Main Bazaar as the oldest thoroughfare now deals in trendy antique wares. The old *tambang* criss-crossing the river are motorized, and besides carrying passengers, carry advertisements too. Where steamships used to call at the godowns lining the embankment, international houseboats now berth for a landed holiday. This embankment, further strengthened against the tidal changes, has been transformed into a pleasant esplanade called the Waterfront. A living diorama of the town's history is featured along its walkway from Pangkalan Batu to the Padungan junction. The Hilton chain's hotel stands on the former Borneo Company site, and competes for prominence with Fort Margherita and its silent canons across the river.

Kuching picked up the new trade of eco-tourism in the 1980s. Gone are the days of government lodgings and resthouses for accommodation. Highrise hotels have taken their place. Yet, among the mementos visitors take away are old Kuching's romantic, historical memories, etched deeply in its mountains, rivers, streets and buildings, and most of all, its people. In short, the distinctive character of the people remains, untouched by the urban spells of the town.

# Bibliography

Abang Yusuf bin Abang Puteh, *Some Aspects of the Marriage Customs among the Sarawak Malays*, Kuala Lumpur, Dewan Bahasa dan Pustaka, 1966.

Appell, George, 'The Journal of James Austin Wilder during His Visit to Sarawak in 1896, Part I', *Sarawak Museum Journal*, Vol. XVI, Nos. 32–33 (New Series), July–December 1968, pp. 407–34.

———, 'The Journal of James Austin Wilder during His Visit to Sarawak in 1896, Part II', *Sarawak Museum Journal*, Vol. XVII, Nos. 34–35 (New Series), July–December 1969, pp. 315–35.

Archer, John B., 'Many Years Ago', *Sarawak Gazette*, 2 January 1948.

Baring-Gould, S. and Bampfylde, C. A., *History of Sarawak under Its Two White Rajahs, 1839–1908*, London, Henry Sotheran & Co., 1909; reprinted Singapore, Oxford University Press, 1988.

Boyle, Frederick, *Adventures among the Dayaks of Borneo*, London, Hurst and Blackett, 1865.

Brooke, Anthony, *The Facts about Sarawak: A Documentary Account of the Cession to Britain in 1946*, Singapore, Summertime Press, 1983.

Brooke, Sir Charles A. J., *Ten Years in Sarawak*, 2 vols., London, Tinsley Brothers, 1866; reprinted Singapore, Oxford University Press, 1989.

Brooke, Sir James, *A Letter from Borneo, with Notices of the Country and Its Inhabitants*, London, L. & G. Seeley, 1842.

Brooke, Margaret, *My Life in Sarawak*, London, Methuen, 1913; reprinted Singapore, Oxford University Press, 1986.

Brooke, Sylvia, *Queen of the Headhunters: The Autobiography of H. H. the Hon. Sylvia Lady Brooke, Ranee of Sarawak*, London, Sidwick & Jackson, 1970; reprinted Oxford University Press, 1990.

———, *Sylvia of Sarawak: An Autobiography, by H. H. the Ranee of Sarawak*, London, Hutchinson, 1936.

Chang, Pat Poh, 'Bau Chinese Rebellion 1857', *Sarawak Gazette*, April 1986, pp. 34–44.

———, 'Kuching: Is It Really a Cat City?', *Sarawak Gazette*, Vol. CXVIII, No. 1515, April 1991.

Chater, W. J., *Sarawak Long Ago*, Kuching, Borneo Literature Bureau, 1969.

Chin, John M., *The Sarawak Chinese*, Kuala Lumpur, Oxford University Press, 1981.

Christie, Ella, 'The First Tourist: Astana Guest, Kuchin, 1904', *Sarawak Museum Journal*, Vol. X, Nos. 17-18 (New Series), July–December 1961, pp. 43–9.

Crisswell, Colin N., *Rajah Charles Brooke: Monarch of All He Surveyed*, Kuala Lumpur, Oxford University Press, 1978.

Dickson, M. G. (comp.), *A Sarawak Anthology*, London, University of London Press Limited, 1965.

Geddes, W. R., *Nine Dayak Nights*, London, Oxford University Press, 1961.

Gullick, J. M., *Malaysia and Its Neighbours*, London, Routledge & Kegan Paul, 1967.

Harrison, Tom, *The Malays of South-West Sarawak before Malaysia: A Socio-Ecological Survey*, London, Macmillan, 1970.

_____ (ed.), *The Peoples of Sarawak*, Kuching, Government Printing Office, 1959.

Helms, Ludvig Verner, *Pioneering in the Far East, and Journeys to California in 1849, and to the White Sea in 1878*, London, W. H. Allen, 1882.

Hornaday, William T., *Two Years in the Jungle: The Experiences of a Hunter and Naturalist in India, Ceylon, the Malay Peninsula and Borneo*, London, Kegan, Paul, Trench & Co., 1885.

Hose, Charles, *Natural Man: A Record from Borneo*, London, Macmillan, 1926.

Irwin, Graham, *Nineteenth Century Borneo*, Singapore, Donald Moore Books, 1955.

Jackson, James C., *Sarawak: A Geographical Survey of a Developing State*, London, University of London Press, 1968.

Keppel, Henry, *The Expedition to Borneo of HMS Dido for the Suppression of Piracy: With Extracts from the Journal of James Brooke, Esq., of Sarawak, (Now Her Majesty's Commissioner and Consul-General to the Sultan and Independent Chiefs of Borneo), Third Edition, with an Additional Chapter, Comprising Recent Intelligence, by Walter K. Kelly*, 2 vols., London, Chapman and Hall, 1853.

King, Victor T., *The Peoples of Borneo*, Oxford, Blackwell, 1993.

Lo, Joan, *Glimpses from Sarawak's Past*, Kuching, Agas (S) Sdn. Bhd., 1986.

Lockard, Craig Alan, 'Charles Brooke and the Foundations of the Modern Chinese Community in Sarawak, 1863–1917', *Sarawak Museum Journal*, Vol. XIX, Nos. 38–39 (New Series), July–December 1971, pp. 77–108.

————, 'From Kampung to City: A Social History of Kuching, Malaysia, 1820–1970', Ohio University Centre for International Studies, Centre for Southeast Asian Studies, Monographs in International Studies Southeast Asia Series, No. 75, Athens, Ohio,1987.

Low, Hugh, *Sarawak, Its Inhabitants and Productions: Being Notes during a Residence in that Country with H. H. The Rajah Brooke*, London, Richard Bentley, 1848; reprinted Singapore, Oxford University Press, 1988.

MacDonald, Malcolm, *Borneo People*, Singapore, Oxford University Press, 1985.

Marryat, Frank S., *Borneo and the Indian Archipelago, with Drawings of Costumes and Scenery*, London, Longman, Brown, Green and Longmans, 1848.

McDougall, Harriette, *Sketches of Our Life at Sarawak*, London, Society for Promoting Christian Knowledge, 1882; reprinted Singapore, Oxford University Press, 1992.

Munan-Oetelli, Adelheid and Saint, Max, 'The Brooke Burial-ground on the North Side of the River, Kuching', *Sarawak Gazette*, December, 1985.

Mundy, Rodney, *Narratives of Events in Borneo and Celebes, Down to the Occupation of Labuan: From the Journals of James Brooke, Esq., Rajah of Sarawak, and Governor of Labuan. Together with a Narrative of the Operations of H. M. S. Iris*, 2 vols., London, John Murray, 1848.

Payne, Robert, *The White Rajahs of Sarawak*, London, Robert Hale Limited, 1960; reprinted Kuala Lumpur, Oxford University Press, 1986.

Pollard, Elizabeth, *Kuching Past and Present*, Kuching, Borneo Literature Bureau, 1972.

Pringle, Robert, *Rajahs and Rebels: The Ibans of Sarawak under Brooke Rule, 1841–1941*, London, Macmillan, 1970.

Reece, R. H. W., *The Name of Brooke: The End of White Rajah Rule in Sarawak*, Kuala Lumpur, Oxford University Press, 1982.

Reid, Anthony, *Southeast Asia in the Age of Commerce*, New Haven, Yale University Press, 1988, Vol. 1: *The Lands below the Winds*.

Roth, Henry Ling, *The Natives of Sarawak and British North Borneo*, 2 vols., London, Truslove & Hanson, 1896; reprinted Kuala Lumpur, University of Malaya, 1968.

Runciman, Steven, *The White Rajahs: A History of Sarawak*, Kuala Lumpur, S. Abdul Majeed & Co., 1992.

Rutter, Owen, *The Pirate Wind: Tales of the Sea-Robbers of Malaya*, Singapore, Oxford University Press, 1986.

Saint, Max, *Twenty Years in Sarawak, 1848–68, A Flourish for the Bishop and Brooke's Friend Grant*, Kuala Lumpur, S. Abdul Majeed & Co., 1992.

Saunders, Graham, *Bishops and Brookes: The Anglican Mission and the Brooke Raj in Sarawak, 1848–1941*, Singapore, Oxford University Press, 1992.

_____, *A History of Brunei*, Kuala Lumpur, Oxford University Press, 1994.

St John, Spenser, *The Life of Sir James Brooke, The Rajah of Sarawak*, Kuala Lumpur, Oxford University Press, 1994.

Tarling, Nicholas, *The Burthen, the Risk, and the Glory: A Biography of Sir James Brooke*, Kuala Lumpur, Oxford University Press, 1982.

_____, *Britain, the Brookes and Brunei*, Kuala Lumpur, Oxford University Press, 1982.

Tate, D. J. M., *Rajah Brooke's Borneo, The Nineteenth Century World of Pirates and Headhunters, Orang Utan and Hornbills, and Other Such Rarities as Seen through The Illustrated London News and Other Contemporary Sources*, Hong Kong, John Nicholson Ltd., 1988.

Taylor, Brian, 'The Chinese Revolt', *Sarawak Museum Journal*, Vol. XVII, Nos. 34–35, (New Series), July–December 1969, pp. 290–3.

Taylor, Brian and Heyward, Pamela Mildmay, *The Kuching Anglican Schools 1848–1973*, Kuching, Lee Ming Press, 1973.

Templer, John C. (ed.), *The Private Letters of Sir James Brooke, K. C. B., Rajah of Sarawak, Narrating the Events of His Life from 1838 to the Present Time*, 3 vols., London, Richard Bentley, 1853.

Tien, Ju-K'ang, *The Chinese of Sarawak: A Study of Social Structure*, Department of Antropology, The London School of Economics and Political Science, Monographs on Social Anthropology, No. 12, London, 1853.

Wallace, Alfred Russel, *The Malay Archipelago*, reprint of the 1922 edition, Singapore, Graham Brash, 1983.

Ward, Arthur B., *Rajah's Servant*, Cornell University Southeast Asia Program Data Paper No. 61, Ithaca, New York,1966.

Warren, James Francis, *Rikshaw Coolie: A People's History of Singapore (1880–1940)*, Singapore, Oxford University Press, 1986.

Contemporary writing in the *Sarawak Gazette* and the *Sarawak Museum Journal* have also provided material.

# Index

*References in brackets refer to Plate numbers; those in brackets and italics to Colour Plate numbers.*

Sungei Bedil Kecil, 11
Sungei Gartak, 12, 22, 23, 35, 66
Sungei Kuching, 10, 13
Sunni, 12
Supreme Council, 32, 43
Swatow, 54; *see also* Chinese

*TAMBANG*, 17, 29
Tamils, 42, 43, 60, 61, 67; *see also*
Indians
Telecommunications, 43
Temples, 67
Teochew, 14, 16, 30, 33, 36, 49, 52,
54; *see also* Chinese
*Towkays*, 36, 38, 39, 55
Tua Pek Kong Temple, 10, 13, 42,
67, (*14*), (*18*); *see also* Temples
Tuan Muda, 23, 25, 27

*Tukang air*, 22
Tun Haji Abdul Rahman Yakub
Bridge, 70

UPPER CHINA STREET, 22, 33, 49

VALAMBROSA, *see* Resthouses
WALLACE, ALFRED RUSSEL, 46, 64,
68
Ward, Arthur, 30, 47, 63
Waterfront, 71
Wayang Street, 67
Wilder, James Austin, 35, 47

XIAN TIEN SHAN TI, *see* Temples

ZHAOZHOU, 54

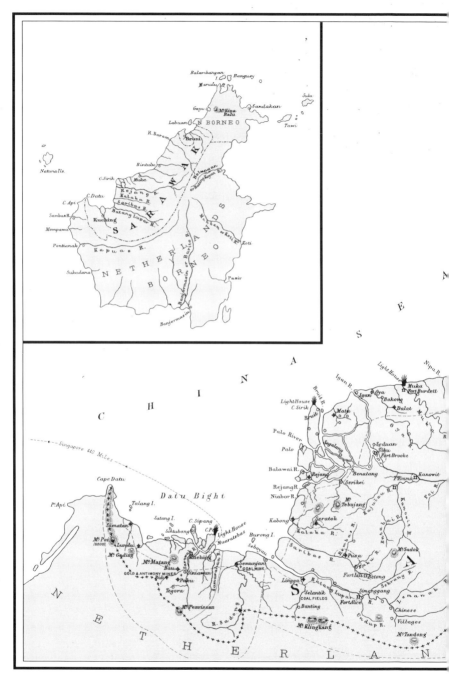

*Source*: Adapted from S. Baring-Gould and C. A. Bampfylde, *A History of Sarawak Under Its Two White Rajahs 1839-1908*, London, Henry Sotheran, 1909.